Finding Sophia

*Nicole Julienne Hall*

Emily
I so hope you enjoy
these characters! And
write, do it you can. Then
let me know ——————>

Nicole Hall

# Contents

*For my Mom*

## Preface

I stared into the streak free mirror and did not recognize the reflection. I think it was me; it just didn't look like me. There was no connection between me and her. I felt nothing when I looked at the image. She seemed a different entity entirely. Her smile was set in a thin line, her face a perfect cream with makeup expertly applied, and her blonde hair brushed perfectly straight. She had pearl earrings that I had never seen before, and they coordinated with the pearl necklace that rested on her modest chest. Well, that I was accustomed to at least. As I surveyed the stranger, I realized that she was pretty. This reflection looked like a cross between a doll and me. It was disconcerting. Where was my signature hairdo or beaming smile? I looked into the reflection's glassy eyes and thought I saw a familiar spark buried deep within. I was leaning into to examine the spark closer when it went dark-like a flame being extinguished-and my body went cold.

## Beginning

I stepped into the breakfast nook and there may have been an audible sound as the gears in my mother's brain processed the image of me dressed for school. I swear each morning she dreaded seeing what I would dress in and silently wished she had sent me to private school where uniforms were required. To her credit though she rarely offered criticism. Or maybe I was wrong. Perhaps she secretly envied the daring I had to wear whatever pleased me regardless of current trends. Today I was wearing baggy jeans that hung long on my petite frame, a thrift store Izod shirt sagging where my breasts would hopefully be in the future, and a multicolored homemade noodle necklace. Really it wasn't so bizarre, but I had topped it off with my favorite hair style; my dirty blonde hair was tied up in eight mini buns randomly fixed to my head with multicolored hair clips.

My mom's style, on the other hand, shouted average but in a contented way. She was 5-6 which gave me hope though I had never considered my short stature a negative. Her hair was shoulder length and brown, her skin just beginning to show signs of age, and her frame was wrapped in the same cardigan and khakis she wore at my tenth birthday. That wouldn't have been so bad, but I was ten almost 6 years ago. Now I was counting down the last 25 days until freedom was mine in the form of a driver's license.

Anyway, I grabbed a granola bar and was holding it in my teeth as I laced my high tops. Mom tossed my jacket on the floor next to me hoping I would finally succumb and wear it. I swallowed a big bite and hung the coat back on its hook. It didn't matter to me that it was freakishly cold for September 2.

I sprinted from the front door to the car and started the engine from the passenger seat while mom finished in the house. I looked across the street from our two-story Craftsmen style home with its front porch supported by wide angular columns at the neighbor's kid waiting for the bus. She was eight and packaged in so many winter clothes it made me think of an old movie where the younger brother whines in a classic line, "I can't put my arms down."

I was laughing as my mom climbed in the car. "What?" She asked defensively.

I pointed across the street at the pitiful kid.

"That's not nice," she said, suppressing a smile knowing exactly what I was referring to.

She drove down the street and we passed multiple for sale signs set in front of vacant lots that were dominated by trees. We had lived in Delaware, on this street, and in this house for as long as I can remember. We moved here when I was three because my dad had opened a surveying office. He was sure that with all the beach front property Delaware would offer lots of opportunities for residential and commercial development. He had been right, too. Mom had stayed at home with me until a few years ago when she started helping out in my dad's office. It amazed me that they could spend so much time together and still enjoy each other's company.

"Sophia, are you excited for your first day?" Mom asked animatedly. My given name was actually Annasophia. Mom had thought it sounded poetic. I always knew when she was pissed because she would address me with the whole mouthful. Also, it was usually delivered in a tone one octave low of shouting. She was pretty easy to read.

"Sure." I was fiddling with the car radio.

"You'll do great."

I shrugged. School had never been too challenging and even the fact that this year I was enrolled in all the College Prep courses did not overly concern me. I was more apprehensive about which other students would be in them than how difficult the course work would be. As far as I knew none of my friends had opted to take the advanced courses. I didn't know if that was by choice or if the opportunity hadn't been offered. Learning and education were secondary to the social benefits of high school for the majority of my friends. We were by no means brainless bimbos; we were just like the remainder of the student body who valued movies over math. My mom had pushed me to take college prep, though, explaining it would save us a lot of money. Each course I received a passing grade in would transfer as college credits.

There were four courses available in the junior year: social studies, English, history, and math. In addition to them I was taking French. I was confident enough in my book smarts that I was sure I would make out fine.

I zeroed in on the clock.

"You should be there right on time," my mom said, answering my unspoken question. Of course, we would be. My mother never arrived anywhere late. On the rare occasion she was a few minutes behind picking me up, bizarre scenarios of her quickly filled my imagination. I would have welcomed one of those rare occasions of being late today. I was already going to be in the "smart class" I didn't want to be the first kid at my desk as well. That screamed "nerd".

I lingered in the hallways long enough that by the time I entered first period, the room was practically full. Now I would know who would be in the classes with me. Not surprisingly, I didn't spot any of my close friends, but that was just me clinging to desperate hope. If any of my them were in these classes, I would have already known. I picked an open seat toward the back and readied my brain for the onslaught.

We were halfway through the syllabus when the classroom

door opened again and Robert Warren walked in with his freshly shaved bald head leading the way. He went straight to the teacher and apologized for his "tardiness." He was so confident and formal that I thought she was going to say it was her fault for starting without him. I didn't know him that well, but we were friendly enough. I noticed his manicured appearance and wondered if his lateness resulted from having to starch his crisp shirt. I giggled softly to myself and he looked over as he passed before taking the empty seat directly behind me.

The teacher picked up right where she had left off as Robert poked my shoulder. "What page are we on?"

"Four." I answered him without turning around.

"It's a bad sign when your class syllabus is so lengthy it needs page numbers," he replied.

I smiled to myself and went back to listening to all the assignments we would have to complete during the first semester. Robert was right. It did sound like an awful lot.

I cringed through four more syllabuses during the school day as my teachers reviewed them in painstaking detail. I was fearing that my social calendar was going to suffer some serious hits due to the heavy assignment load. It was all but forgotten though when the sun hit my face as I exited the building and walked toward the parking lot after math, my last class of the day. The phrase "save the best for last" definitely did not apply. Math had always been my nemesis.

As I moved deeper into the parking l lot I noted a small group corralled around my best friend's new Jeep. As I got closer I noticed the group was all guys with my other best friend Jackie drowning in the midst as they questioned Jen about her tires and lift. I was sure that if she was driving a Pinto there would still be a mass of boys swarming about. The vehicle was just an excuse.

"Hey, Sophia. Ready?" Jen asked turning her full attention to me.

"Uh. Yup." I am not sure what I was agreeing to, but if it meant she was driving and I wouldn't have to call my mom for a ride home, I was all for it. I climbed in the back and Jackie followed me, situating herself in the passenger seat.

She turned around to me, relieved: "Glad you made it out when you did. I was afraid they were going to persuade Jen to open the hood so they could inspect it."

"Ha. She would have to find the manual to figure out how." We laughed together.

Jen climbed in, waving bye to her adoring fans through the window. She was pulling out of the parking spot when I noticed Robert. He stuck out like a sore thumb in his pressed shirt among the other boys who looked like their shirts hadn't been washed recently let alone ironed.

"So, where are we going?" I asked.

"Pharmacy. I need some new nail polish. You guys need to go anywhere?"

"Nope." Jackie and I answered in unison.

Jen, Jackie, and I could have fun together in a jail cell probably. Though hopefully that theory would never be put to the test. If you had to categorize us, Jen was the pretty one, I was the quirky brainy one, and Jackie was the boy crazy one.

Jen was always perfectly put together, I swear she could stick her finger in a light socket in the morning and her hair would still look perfectly placed. Not to say she was shallow, she just happened to be effortlessly pretty. She had moved here in junior high, and our friendship had always been easy.

Jackie was attractive in a different way. Freckles spotted the tops of her cheeks and nose, and she had her wiry full hair tamed back with a headband. Our families were close and we have countless pictures of us growing up. As a result we could get into heated fights, but we were more like family so eventually we worked it out. She was like the sister I didn't have.

The best part of Jen's new wheels was the sound system so we plugged in our favorite playlist and bumped the music, thinking we were cool as we drove across town.

In the pharmacy Jen scrutinized nail polishes she had lined up on the carpet. Jackie looked weary watching her. I think she was afraid we might get kicked out due to Jen's rearranging.

I started weaving through the other aisles. I knew from experience she would be another ten minutes before she made a final choice. I grabbed a handful of gummy hamburgers from the candy

12

aisle and headed to check out.  Apparently everyone else in the store wanted to check out at that particular time also because four other people fell into line as the counter came into view.  I fumbled with the plastic wrapper on one of the burgers when the lady in front of me turned to give me the evil eye.

I never got why my parents said not to eat the food before paying.  I was already in line.  Was it my fault there was only one checker and my stomach was growling?  I looked straight at her, popped it in my mouth, and gave her a big grin.  She turned around, probably contemplating the disgrace American youth reflects on our society.  When I reached the counter, I tossed the last packaged burger on it along with the empty wrappers, purple polish, and impulsively pulled over a pink Barbie camera that a little girl was made to leave.

I walked back to the where Jen and Jackie were trying to find the right spots for the twenty or so colors she had pulled out in search of the perfect pink.  I reached for my new camera and started taking pictures of them.

"Why don't you help instead of documenting the process?" Jackie asked.

"You guys are doing such an awesome job."  I said with sarcasm. Jen glared with her face twisted in annoyance. "Oh,  I missed that shot.  Will you do it again?"  I pressed.

## Friends

You know when you're in school and its accepted to collectively hang out together but there is really only a few people you know well enough to talk to outside the group?  That was us. He was funny, brainy, often sarcastic, and always impeccably dressed (especially for a 16 year old black kid).  He rocked a pink, pressed, polo without a qualm and no one thought twice about it.  It was just cute, not eccentric because he was too confident with his image.  In reality he was probably more comfortable with his own identity than most adults twice his age.  Anyway that was Robert. We had had mutual friends throughout high school and attended similar after school and weekend outings.

Our friendship was tightened in the last few weeks after finding ourselves in all the College Prep courses together.  This set us apart from the majority of our friends though we kept our nerd profile as low status as we could. It was after a particularly grueling lecture in social studies that Robert approached me.

"Hot." Was his random comment as we filed out of class him closely trailing behind me.

Huh…I never thought he had really looked twice at me in that way. I turned and I eyed him with a flirty grin, just out of reflex. I *was* a hormone filled teenager.

"Hot." He repeated as he gestured toward my best friend Jen.

She was waiting for me outside class. No shit I thought, everyone thinks so. It wasn't always easy being best friends with one of the most popular girls in school.

My face quickly reorganized to a smile suppressing a scowl. "Uh huh." Was my unenthused reply. It wasn't that I was into him it just would have been nice for him to be into me. There is an instant ego boost when someone you hadn't really considered found you attractive.

"Call me tonight, okay?" He was still ogling her all while slipping his phone number into the notebook I had clutched to my chest.

What an invitation, I thought sarcastically. I didn't respond. Instead I hitched my arm into Jen's and walked down the hall to lunch.

"So how are we celebrating the big day?" Jen asked vaguely.

"I suppose that depends on what we are celebrating?" I answered just as Jackie closed ranks so that I was sandwiched in the middle of them.

"We can celebrate the hot new uniforms the wrestling team just ordered?" She chuckled alone. It was not uncommon for her to be the only person laughing at her jokes but it never seemed to faze her.

"I could care less about what lycra suits the boys will be wearing while they grope at each other and people yell at them where to touch and grab their opponent." Jen responded. "I was alluding to your birthday on Saturday when you will be officially indoctrinated to the driving populace."

"That sounds worthwhile." Jackie agreed and swung her hip into mine causing my step to falter just as we entered the lunch room.

"It's no fun if I have to organize the plans. You guys just tell me the location and I will be there." I answered.

Freakin homework. I muttered to myself later that nights as I pulled out my social studies textbook. I was rifling through my backpack in a frustrated harsh way when a slip of paper caught itself between my comforter and headboard. I quickly pinched it between my fingers before it could fall behind the abyss that lay beyond my mattress. My room wasn't what you would call messy or neat. Its category lay somewhere in the gray area between. For some ungodly reason my mom had let me choose the colors when I was eight or something so the walls alternated in color from orange to purple. I was finding it hard to concentrate with the colors blaring at me. I had done my best to cover a portion, and my movie posters did provide some refuge from the colors but it was still hideous.

I adjusted the paper in my fingers so it was upright. Seven digits stared back at me and it was a brief second before I remembered Robert's enamored face focused on Jen as he wedged it into my notebook earlier in the day.

Hmm. Do I really feel like listening to an hour of how amazing and beautiful my best friend is, again! I thought to myself. It was better then starting my stupid homework; and the test wasn't for a week. I had adequately convinced myself so I dialed his number.

I threw myself backwards onto my puffy comforter when a formal female "Hello" broke through the phone line and surprised me.

My thoughts scattered…"uh is Robert available?"

There was a lengthy pause and then "S'uuuup." Was the indifferent greeting I received from the familiar deep voice.

The conversation progressed smoothly. He was easy to talk to, probably because we had no pretenses with each other and knew that there was no interest besides friendship.

It wasn't awkward for any moment. We never even got around to the topic of Jen before we were interrupted on his side of the line. *Bedtime,* coming from a parental tone was all I heard.

"Alright, I gotta go." He said  Jeez, he succumbed so easily.

"K, See you tomorrow".

It  had not been the conversation I was expecting to endure.

I had actually enjoyed talking to him. It was nice to complain about the teachers and classes we were taking. Plus, it had beat doing homework.

My eyes drifted across the lunch table as I approached so I could preselect a seat in my mind. I glanced around and spotted Robert consumed in conversation, and, sporting another perfectly pressed button down. He was squeezed between Jen and Jackie.

Something in my chest dipped slightly when I watched him smile at Jen and I made a bee line for the seat across from Jackie. I turned my body around to drape my backpack on the seat.

"Ow." I growled massaging my calf where someone had kicked me.

Robert's eyebrows arched and a menacing smile snuck onto his face.

"What's the assault for?" I accused

"Sorry, I had to get off the phone last night…" a few heads turned in our direction "my mom is annoyingly strict."

"It's cool." I offered casually. I could tell in my peripheral vision that Jen was trying to make eye contact so I turned toward her. A question was boring through her eyes. I just shrugged a bit and tilted my head slightly to the side to illustrate there was no story to share.

At the end of lunch, I was carrying my tray across the cafeteria to dump it when Jen raced up to me. She was carrying my backpack in her free hand signaling that we were walking together to French class. Now.

"You didn't tell me Robert called you last night!" She blurted.

"He didn't" I corrected. "I called him."

"Oh, do you like him?"

"It's not like that." I explained.

"Well, why did you call him then? Seems kinda out of nowhere."

"He slipped his number in my notebook yesterday when we were leaving social studies." I was forcing her to pull every detail out of me. I was offering nothing.

"Do you think he likes you?" Her eyes tightened.

Ugh. For some reason I didn't want to enlighten Jen to the fact that the catalyst for our call had actually been her but it was inevitable unless I was going to lie and there really was no reason for that.

"I think he has a thing for you, actually." My shoulders dipped, I was tired of twenty questions. I may as well confess "He said he thought you were hot."

"Really?" She beamed.

This sucked. It wasn't that I liked him. It was that he liked her. I really didn't feel like recapping the entire phone call for her enjoyment. We never talked about her anyway so I am sure the details would be of no interest. Our forced silence was ended abruptly by the bell and Jen didn't miss a beat jumping back into our conversation.

"What did he say?" I could tell she was hoping for juicy details.

"We just talked about random stuff. He never even got into mentioning you." Sorry to disappoint but I wasn't going to sugar coat it for her.

We turned the corner toward my English class and I noticed a single flutter in my stomach. Why was I suddenly nervous to see him? His absence or presence in our shared classes had been of no consequence to me over the last few weeks but now all of a sudden he shows interest in Jen and I am acting stupid?

I tried to suppress my smile as he came into view but it was impossible. I probably looked ridiculous beaming in his direction where he was leaning with his back to the wall outside of class and looking toward Jen. Or was he?

Our eyes met for a half second before I noticed Jen waving flirtatiously at him and his gaze shifted. Gag me. I broke from our synchronized stride, walked past Robert, and went straight to my desk.

During class I tried to concentrate on anything but the fact that he was sitting directly behind me but for some reason the realization consumed me. What was my problem? He had sat there for the last four weeks totaling 20 days minus a school holiday and one of my absences. This meant that for 18 days he had sat behind me staring past my head listening to the teacher and I had not considered every adjustment I made in my seat. This was pathetic. Maybe it is the law of attraction that what you can't have you invariably desire. I tried to hold as still as possible without coming off as a stone freak. You know move just enough to appear relaxed when in actuality each move was absurdly calculated.

I took a calming breath as I packed my pencil and textbook into my backpack, thankful that class and school were over. The freaking zipper was stuck…shit. I yanked it and everything I had just shoved in tumbled out. Why when I am trying so fiercely to not draw attention to myself does the universe conspire for the exact opposite to occur? Someone up there must be laughing their ass off. I hope you are enjoying this. I thought sarcastically.

"Maybe you should treat your belongings with more respect." Robert's cool voice broke through the silent scolding I was giving myself.

I glared up from the floor where I was haphazardly cramming things into my bag…as quickly as possible.

"Jeez. You could physically hurt someone with that face. Seriously, stop looking at me like that." He held out his hand and I passed him my traitor of a book bag.

"I guess I don't feel like smiling and giggling at you like some other people." I did my best impression of Jen's pre-class greeting.

Chuckling at my obvious irritation, he smoothly adjusted the zipper and organized the items I had stuffed in.

I started again. "I am just annoyed I was looking forward to the football game this weekend and now I have to start reading Jane Eyre." I explained calmly. It seemed that I was either beaming or scowling at him today.

Just then some of his friends barged into the room to collect him. One of them had thrown an arm around his neck and was yanking him out the door. He passed me the book bag and mimicked a phone with his hand, mouthing call me. My stomach leaped.

The big dinner of mashed potatoes and pork chops digesting in my stomach was making me sleepy and the view of all my homework splayed out on my bed was angering me. I glanced at my cell phone for easily the third time in the last hour. I was not going to call him. Everybody's attention at the lunch table was piqued today with our one conversation. I didn't want to get their imaginations stirring needlessly again.

It was approaching 9 PM when I had finally finished everything I needed to. My eyes locked on the worn black book that looked to be a hundred years old. In reality the story of Jane Eyre was a hundred years old, but my copy from the library wasn't much older than I. I considered the state of its wear and consoled myself that any book with that level of deterioration couldn't be too unpleasant.

As I picked it up to begin examining it closer, I saw my cell phone light up and heard the muffled noise it makes when vibrating. A surge shot through my body. And then a smile took over my face when I recognized the number.

"Hello." I said trying to sound nonchalant when I was

seriously thrilled for no logical reason that he had called me.

"Hey is this Jen, uh…I mean Sophia?" Oh, joy just the greeting I was hoping for. The momentary surge of energy quickly evaporated and was instantly replaced with a simmering.

I heard cackling on his side of the line. He was enjoying himself.

"You are such an ass."

"Did I hurt your feelings?" I swear he just couldn't help teasing me. He sounded so amused and I couldn't stay mad at him. It was kind of annoying.

"Isn't it past your bedtime? I mean you must have to get up early to press your shirts so perfectly before school." I chided.

"You noticed how I dress, huh?" He responded cooly.

"Well, your style significantly differs from the posse you were dragged out by earlier today." I sneered back.

"I stand out to your discerning eye, do I?" He inhaled. "I don't think this assessment will surprise you, but your look is atypical from the general student body as well."

"Ok, I will concede that point." I wasn't sure how I felt about that comment, but before I could ponder its implication, he was on to the next topic.

The conversation continued to flow similar to the previous night but with a new edge to it as well. We were getting more familiar with one another and our remarks were heavily laden with sarcasm and teasing. Really we just bantered back and forth and all too soon I realized it was 1 a.m..

"Holy crap! Your mom forgot to tell us it was bedtime." I joked.

"Ha. She had already given her warning before I called you. I should go to bed though. The iron beckons all too early."

"Me too. I am spent. Night."

"See you tomorrow." I hung up the phone and clutched it to my chest.

I had been completely lying when I said I was tired. I had been on my toes for the last few hours, responding to his teasing comments with witty remarks. Now I let myself relax and review all that had passed between us. I examined each of his words, tone, and even considered his pauses.

I was allowing myself to be enamored by him while I was in the solace of my darkened room. It was strange how quickly I had become charmed by him. It wasn't as if I hadn't known him for the last two years. We had gone to movies, football games, field trips together with our friends but now I felt so different around him. I wondered if he felt anything different too? Or was he still trying to get to Jen?

What would ensue tomorrow at school was a mystery that kept me reeling for the next while until at some point I unwillingly fell asleep.

Knock, knock. An unwelcome sound that I determined to be my mom's wake up call roused me from my too short sleep. I sat up dazedly and realized my school work was still covering my bed and

I had literally slept on some of my papers. The late night phone call flooded my thoughts. Then realizing how late I actually was I sprang out of bed and flew through my morning routine. I finished putting my farmer style twin braids in and was ironing out my crumpled papers with my hands as I choked down a granola bar. I didn't have a chance to register my mom's reaction to my outfit today…it consisted of a black fitted hooded shirt, an acceptable length skirt, and pink tights tucked into my black Uggs.

As my mom pulled up to the school's main entrance I nonchalantly surveyed the school parking lot. It came to my attention that after this weekend I would be legally permitted to drive myself to school. Thank you Jesus.

"Looking for Jen?" I guess I wasn't being as discreet as I thought

"Uh, no…err yea." Agreeing was easier than explaining I had been suddenly overcome with an infatuation for a guy I had known for the last two years.

I spotted him. He was laughing and carrying on with his said posse. His preppy v-neck sweater stood out from the baggy jeans and over sized tees his friends wore. His friends seemed to have taken the same oath as me and were not wearing coats.

I inhaled sharply and stepped out of the car. I went straight to class telling myself I could lumber through a few pages of Jane Eyre before class started. If I was being honest with myself, I really just wanted to be there to meet Robert as soon as possible. The class started to fill and he slid into his seat with not a second to spare. He looked at me and made an exaggerated sleepy face. This made my stomach leap and I mouthed back "I know."

After class he waited outside the door for me in an obvious way, not trying to hide his intentions. His messenger bag was slung across his chest and his shoulder was pressed to the wall. He stood a couple feet from the doorway as I exited. He was gorgeous.

"Not enough time for the iron?" I pointed to his sweater as I approached his poised figure.

"Nope." He gave me a knowing look and tugged one of my braids. "Not enough time for the buns."

"Nope."

"It's cute." My stomach leaped again. His compliment caught me off guard and I couldn't formulate a response with my usual promptness.

"What no retort?"

I rolled my eyes.

"This may be a record. You have been silent for an extended period of time." I stalked off. He caught up and grasped my arm. "What? Did I exhaust all your wit with our lengthy conversation last night?"

"No. You just seemed so amused by my silence I didn't want to ruin your fun." I tossed back.

"Hmm." Amusement continued to color his always collected face. He was so pulled together. His clothes, mannerisms, remarks were never agitated. He seemed to exist in a constant state of ease. It was irksome. Why wasn't he awkward and confused like every other teenager on earth?  How was it that he was so secure with himself?  Not to say that I was lost and dubious by any means but I didn't exude self assuredness with every breath either.

I woke up that Saturday morning and immediately looked out my window to make sure forces of nature had not ruined my birthday by causing a tree to land on my ticket to freedom.  I was relieved to see the slightly abused silver four door manual transmission Honda parked in the exact spot as when I had gone to bed last night.  And with no new damage.  I had busted my ass all summer helping with anything and everything at my dad's office so that I could buy it.  I had painted, mowed, and cleaned every inch of the property and it was all going to pay off now.

My mom laughed from where she was standing at the sink in the kitchen when I flew down the stairs already dressed at seven in the morning and ran out the front door.  I was going to go get coffee by myself, in my car.  Did I mention I was going to go by myself, in my car?  I pulled up on the door handle but it didn't open.  I knew somehow the universe would conspire against me today.  *Crap.*  I tried the door again, then noting it was locked, I turned around.  My shoulders fell and I slinked back toward the house where my mom and dad stood at the door laughing at me.

"Did they forget to teach you about the importance of keys in driver's ed?"  My dad teased and tossed me a horribly wrapped package.  It looked like someone had sat on it which surely meant my mom had let him take care of the wrapping.

The wrinkled mess made a clinking sound when I caught it in my hands. I tore the paper off like a toddler on Christmas morning and found my car keys with some surprise accoutrements. There was a mini tube of Mace, a whistle, a led flashlight, and the fattest keychain I had ever seen. It was practically an entire stuffed animal. I rolled my eyes and could tell they were enjoying my reaction.

"You couldn't find a tazer to fit on the key ring?" I questioned.

"Just wanted to make sure you have everything you need." Dad answered seriously.

"And that you wouldn't lose your keys." Mom added pointing to the stuffed animal that was the size of a hamster. It was the hippopotamus character from Richard Scarry's Busy Town, my favorite book when I was four. I was going to need a separate bag just for my keys. Really, though, I wouldn't have cared if they had drilled a hole in an entire tool chest as long as they had handed the keys to me when they were done so I could drive away.

Eventually they both sobered up from their shared enjoyment of watching me examine the asinine key ring, and my mom gave me a lengthy safe driving lecture. After what felt like an eternity but was probably ten minutes she slouched back from the kitchen table signaling that I was free to proceed. That was when our attention was simultaneously drawn to the spastic knocking on the front door.

A moment later Jen and Jackie lunged in unable to wait for admittance. Their enthusiasm matched the excitement I had displayed before the dry and drawn out driving speech had deadened my senses. They each grabbed an arm and pulled me out the door shouting that we were going shopping for the day.

We got bagels and coffee, then drove 45 minutes north to Dover and went to the mall, before heading another 45 minutes north to the top of the state. We wanted to check out, Avalon, a trendy new store.

Upon entering we could see all the local interest had been warranted. Shelves and display tables were filled with designer purses and stiletto heels that you would be more likely to see in a fashion magazine than in our high school. I knew immediately that this place was not going to sell anything in my price range. I would have had better luck at the Salvation Army. Jen on the other hand I thought might permanently change her address so she could live in the fitting room.

"Can I see these in my size too, please?" She batted her eyelashes at the poor guy who was literally on his knees helping her try on shoes. I was tempted to clue him in that she had learned to tie her shoes in kindergarten but kept my lips sealed. The floor encircling her was littered with opened boxes and tissue paper; remnants of a serious shopper.

Bored with her escapades I watched another worker across the store dress a mannequin in a fitted khaki women's two piece suit. I laughed when she topped it off with a fur hood covered in jagged orange and black stripes, a la tiger, complete with ears. Black ribbon hung down on both sides and ended with black fur puffs. I grabbed Jackie's hand and pulled her over to the mannequin.

"Look at this." I showed her the hood. "I love it."

"You would." She said.

I grabbed it down, put it on and looked for a mirror. I checked myself out and decided it was adorable.

It was another twenty minutes before Jen even noticed we were gone. She was walking to the register empty handed because the attendant was carrying the three boxes of shoes she had decided on.

"Oh my god. That is so you." She said pointing to the hood I was *still* wearing.

"I know it's super cute." I took another look in the mirror at myself then placed it back on the mannequin.

"What are you doing?" Jen asked.

I shrugged. I could not afford to spend 35 dollars on a completely useless and unnecessary tiger hood. Where was I going to wear it anyway?

"Let me buy it for your birthday." She said.

Normally I would have protested some but I wanted it so bad that I immediately allowed her to get it for me. I wore it the rest of the day even when we stopped for pizza on our way home. I thoroughly enjoyed each of the weary stares the other patrons gave me.

It was an amazing day. I crawled into bed spent, thankful for my best friends, and laid my tiger hooded head on my pillow.

## Party

On Tuesday I was sitting at the lunch table begging Jackie for some of her mom's homemade blueberry muffin. The term "melt in your mouth" definitely applied. It was a fall tradition. Her mom making them with fresh hand picked blueberries, not me begging for the crumbs.

Simultaneously I was watching Robert with quick glances and brief peeks. He was sitting next to Troy, and they were staring into his iPod shuffling through the songs. Jackie finally caved and passed me half her muffin. Before she could change her mind, I popped the entire chunk into my mouth which was not an easy feat considering Mrs. Walls's muffins are practically the size of a grapefruit. I was struggling trying to swallow it without choking or having to spit part of it out so I would have an amount that was manageable to chew, all while looking cool. Of course that is when Robert cleared his throat loudly to get everyone's attention and locked eyes with me. I couldn't smile due to the massive lump of half chewed muffin occupying my entire mouth. My eyes bugged out in embarrassment and he smiled amusingly. Pretty much everyone was looking in his direction waiting for the announcement to follow his interruption.

"My parents are going to Philadelphia Friday night and said I could throw a party as long as it is relatively small and tame, so tell everyone you know and come over around 9:00."

He went back to staring at Troy's iPod and I saw that they were scribbling on a piece of paper, probably writing down songs. I finally swallowed the muffin and thanked a higher power that I hadn't choked to death in the process.

Jackie, Jen and I were walking to class after lunch and I was thinking about Robert's party. Obviously he was inviting anyone who could get there, but I didn't know if I should go. I wanted to. I wanted to see his house, his room. I had pictured it in my head while we talked on the phone, and I was definitely hoping to sneak a look at it during the party. I was praying Jackie would bring it up, but she was talking about a Senior dance practically six weeks in the future. My interests were more immediate and feasible. The dance was for Seniors only, unless by invitation as a date with an upperclassmen.

I couldn't wait any longer and dived head first when Jackie took a rare pause to breathe. "So what do you think about the party at Robert's?" I asked attempting to douse my curiosity with cavalier.

"I have a cheerleading competition that night. I am going to be gone that whole weekend. Otherwise it sounds like it might have potential." Jen answered.

"I don't know." Ugh. The endless talker had nothing to say. I didn't want to push the subject and totally give myself away but I needed her to go with me.

"Do you want to go? It might be fun?" I shrugged forcing my body language to match my tone.

"Ehh." Was she toying with me? Did she suspect the desperate note I was trying to hide?

"There might be some older guys there. Maybe you could snatch a date for the ball." I gave up on being nonchalant and surrendered myself to transparency. Surely she would detect my enthusiasm and wonder why I wanted to go so bad.

"Ooh. You are always thinking. Good call. We are going." My stomach fluttered. She had taken the bait, hadn't suspected a thing, and the result was we were going to Robert's party at Robert's house tomorrow night. I was practically floating as we walked down the hall.

We sat in the back of class and debated what older guys might be at the party while Mrs. Persons fought with the DVD player. She finally got the movie to play but it did not deter our conversation. We moved from what guys would be there to what we should wear.

We walked into the hall together and said "Au revoir." Then went our separate ways.

I swung open the door to English and immediately observed Robert's seat was still empty. I pretended not to be disappointed but had been looking forward to talking to him before class started. When I took a step into the room, I saw him to the left talking to the teacher at her desk. He didn't seem to notice me and I headed toward my seat. I tried to busy myself rearranging pencils and such in my backpack waiting for him to sit down. He slid into his seat in one smooth motion and leaned toward me.

"You ok?" He asked concerned.

"Uhh, yeah." What was he talking about? Why did I always feel like I was trying to catch up to his conversation?

"It seemed like that muffin was really giving you a run for your money and I wanted to make sure it hadn't done any lasting damage." Could he ever just let things be? Did he have to criticize and mortify me at every opportunity? I narrowed my eyes.

"Really I was mentally reviewing the Heimlich we learned in gym."

"You are supposed to wait for someone to give the choking sign before you do the Heimlich." I put my hands to my throat and demonstrated.

"Just wanted to be prepared if you needed me. I wouldn't want you using your death as an excuse to not come to my party."

"Yes, that would be sooo selfish of me." I turned forward just as the teacher started her lecture.

My stomach was at full flutter Friday evening while I scrutinized every item hanging in my closet and those covering the floor alike. The phone rang somewhere within the pile of shirts and pants and I threw them around the room in haste to dig it out before I missed the call.

"Hey ,Jackie!" My excitement was laughable.

"Hey, Soph. I can't go tonight! I am really sorry. My mom is pissed about the C on my English paper and grounded me for the weekend."

"Oh." Crap. Now I had to go alone or not at all. This sucks.

"Are you still gonna go? You should. Scope out some seniors for us." She encouraged.

"Yeah, I guess I will." I had told Robert last night on the phone if I didn't choke and die between then and now I would be there. He had made me promise that if I did in fact choke and die I would be there posthumously.

I didn't feel as brave now that I was going alone and grabbed for an outfit I would hopefully feel comfortable in. I slipped into my ballet flats, smoothed my wide leg jeans, and adjusted the flowy purple peasant top under my zip up hoodie. I assessed my reflection in the mirror and mentally wished that Jen wasn't out of town.

I pulled into Robert's development and laughed. No wonder he wore Polo shirts all the time. He lived in the Rehoboth Beach Yacht and Country Club. How perfect. I wonder if he plays golf, too. I parked at the end of a long line of cars and walked through

35

the grass up to his house. It was like our house with two stories and a front porch but with a generic feel. It looked like all the other ones I had passed along the road since I pulled into the development.

It was loud and dim inside his house. There was a table at the entrance scattered with highlighters in a variety of colors and tons of glow sticks. I scanned the room and saw that most people had adorned themselves in some way with the provided materials. There were glowing faces, clothes, and hair. It was bizarre but looked fun. I grabbed the pink highlighter and a handful of glow sticks. I painted my nails pink and had my arms raised as I wove the last stick through my hair which was done up in braids and buns. I was jamming it in to be sure it was secure when someone playfully poked my ribs from behind.

"I recognized your hair from across the room." Robert said to my back. I spun around and laughed. His entire mouth-lips, tongue, and teeth-were glowing.

"What did you do? Eat a glow stick? I am pretty sure they are toxic."

"Toxic? Really? I hope you paid better attention than I did in gym on CPR day because I may need your services."

"Seriously, Robert you can't eat those." I was starting to get worried for real.

"I didn't eat a glow stick." He laughed. "It's this mouthwash my cousin brought from a costume shop near his house. Funny, huh? Come on let me introduce you. He is here for the weekend from Georgia. His parents are the reason we are able have this

36

party. They took my parents to Philly tonight for a symphony."

He pulled my arm and I pretended to be annoyed but I was thrilled he had singled me out. The house was packed full of people, and he had picked me to escort around. We walked through the dancing crowd and he bee lined for the screened in porch where it was a little less cramped. We approached a group of three. The girls I recognized from school. I think they were sophomores, but the guy I didn't know. He seemed to be holding his position precariously and I deduced it was a result of whatever alcoholic beverage had filled his cup.

"Ricky, this is my girl Sophia. Sophia this is my cousin Ricky. " He was wearing the traditional baggy pants and oversized tee shirt emblazoned with a brand name. I was surprised they were cousins. Besides their skin color they seemed completely different. There probably wasn't a Polo shirt anywhere in this guy's closet.

"Your girl?" he replied emphasizing the *your*, while gesturing to me with his empty cup. Ricky was small with a cocky vibe. I didn't appreciate the way he examined me.

"Friends," was Robert's succinct response. I would be lying if I said that didn't sting a little but what did I expect. We were just friends.

I tugged at Robert's shirt to break the glare between them. "I'm going to go find your bathroom." I was sure their silent conversation would be easier to finish without my presence. Besides I wanted to sneak a look at his bedroom.

The first door I opened was in fact the bathroom. The

second I hoped was a guest room. It had a floral comforter and a vanity. If this was his, we were in trouble. The last door on the left was definitely Robert's. It was just messy enough to not scream OCD. There was a small TV that occupied a spot on his filled bookshelf. His full sized bed was along the opposite wall and covered carelessly with a grey pinstriped comforter. There were four oversized wood frames with black and white family photos. I walked toward them to get a better look when I heard the door open. I was hoping it was a random guest looking for the bathroom, but it was Ricky. He ambled in my direction.

"Those are from family vacations." He pointed to the photos. "Our parents plan a big one every couple years."

"Oh. That's nice." I smiled and headed for the door. I did not want to be anywhere alone with this guy. He had creep written all over him. I was darting past him when he grabbed my arm.

"What's the hurry?" He pulled me toward him and the alcohol on his breath was pungent. His grip was stronger than I would have expected, and while I reached with my opposite hand to free myself from his grip he pressed his mouth messily onto mine. I leaned backward and tried to push him away from me at the same time. It was enough for him to lose his footing and he staggered to the side. I turned toward the door while he was still pulling on my arm.

Just then the door opened wide and the black light flooded into the room. Robert took in the scene. I could see him register the fear in my eyes and then the glow on my lips that had transferred from Ricky's mouth to mine during the attack. He grabbed Ricky's hand off my arm and pushed him into the bookshelf with controlled anger. A few books fell to the floor. He probably would have left it at that but in Ricky's drunken stupor he pushed back and instigated Robert's fury again. Robert pulled his arm back and slammed his clenched fist into Ricky's face. My mouth fell open.

Ricky crumpled to the floor and Robert turned to me "Are you ok?"

I nodded.

"Let's get out of here." He grabbed his keys off the dresser and we fled out the back door into the darkness. We trekked through the trees to his car and got in silently.

"I am so sorry. Ricky can be a good guy; he is just a dick when he drinks," he apologized.

"Yes. I noticed." I was holding on with both hands to the seatbelt strap crossing my chest.

"Are you ok? You just nodded before. Did he hurt you? Do you want me to take you home?" He offered.

"Yes, I am ok. No, he didn't hurt me. He basically just slobbered on me but it was repulsive. No, I don't really feel like going home yet. I am a little freaked out by it all."

He drove a little ways before pulling into a diner. It was one of the authentic silver bullet jobs. I had passed it before on the highway but had never stopped to eat there. I was shocked to find the parking lot mostly full when the clock was approaching eleven. I guess there weren't too many places to choose from this late at night.

"It's a family favorite." He waited for me to unbuckle my belt first, making sure I was ready to go in. Robert waved to the guy pouring coffee behind the counter and pointed to a booth in the far corner. The man nodded his consent. Robert slunk down into his seat.

"I'm going to use the bathroom, K." I said before sitting down.

"K." He threw back teasingly.

I rolled my eyes.

I squeezed into the teeny bathroom and let the water run until it was hot. I slathered my face with soap and rinsed it thoroughly with the scorching water. I wanted to erase the memory of Ricky from my face and mind. I looked at myself in the mirror. I was a mess. I took my hair out and threw the glow sticks in the trash. With a bobby pin in my mouth I French braided one side of my hair, pinned it in place, and repeated it on the other side. Then I pulled them into a ponytail at the nape of my neck. I dusted my face with powder from my bag and put on a fresh layer of lip gloss. A smile crossed my face, I was here with Robert. Just the two of us. This was better than I could have hoped. I headed out of the bathroom. He was looking in my direction as soon as I came around the corner. He smiled at me as if he was as glad to see me as I was to see him. My heart was light, and I slid into the opposite side of the booth. There was an order of fries and a monster slice of peanut butter pie in the center of the table.

"Is this a family favorite also?" I asked.

"No. We usually come here for breakfast. They have really awesome Belgian waffles." He had a fry in his hand and was using it when he talked for added emphasis.

I took a chunk of the chocolate graham cracker crust and spooned it into my mouth.

"Hold on there. That is the best part. You are supposed to save the crust for last. Besides, didn't you learn your lesson earlier in the week about taking bites bigger than your head. It's dangerous."

"Just make sure you wait until I give you the official choking sign before Heimliching me."

"Heimliching you?" He leaned forward and cocked his head to the side a little. "That sounds naughty." My blood pulsed faster when he said naughty. I found his mannerisms captivating.

"You really amuse yourself don't you?" I said.

"Yup. Especially when it is stirring you." He leaned back, satisfied that his taunting had caused a reaction within me. He was so right. He could falter my breathing pattern simply by looking at me. I broke his gaze and looked to the side.

"Your friend is watching us." I whispered. He looked confused at first but then realized I was referring to the guy behind the counter.

"I am sure he is wondering who you are to me."

As am I. I thought to myself.

"He probably figures we are dating with us being out late

41

and alone on a Friday night."

"Is that from past experience?  Do you take all your girlfriends here?"

"Well, how can a girl not be impressed with this wonderful ambience.  It's always a hit."  He kidded.

"I like it."  I shrugged.

"Yes, but you're not like most girls."  He replied quickly.

"I am not sure if that is good or bad."  I pondered.

"Good.  Definitely good."

We both stared across the table for a moment, studying each other.  A long time later we had finally finished.  I was sure the cleaned plates were a sign of our hesitancy to leave more than actual hunger.

"You want to mess with him a little bit."  He said in a hushed tone.

"Sure."  Whatever he wanted to do sounded fine with me.

He picked up the crumpled piece of paper the waitress had tossed between us while she was whizzing around the tables.  I followed him to the checkout desk and leaned with my back to the wall.  There was a women ahead of Robert paying her bill.  I closed my eyes and tilted my head back, resting on the wall.  My body felt heavy and tired now that his gripping effect had eased off some.

It was late and had been a long evening.  I was ready to crawl into my bed and sleep until noon.  I heard Robert talking to the cashier and then moments later his hand was caressing me as it smoothed down my throat.  His other arm wrapped my torso.

torso. Warmth radiated from his embrace and from where he stood before me. My eyes snapped open and I felt a tingling linger from each spot his fingertips grazed. He flicked his eyes over to the counter, hinting that this was for the benefit of the nosy counter man. This scene was going beyond the flirtatious bubble we usually existed within. That worked for me.

He breathed. "I had a good time tonight." There was an understatement. By some saving grace a partial response formulated in my head and I spewed it out.

"Ehh. It was alright. " He leaned back and I had to stop myself from mirroring his movements that would have kept our bodies inches apart. He smiled warmly and motioned toward the exit.

As we approached the car, he moved ahead to open the door for me. I paused before climbing in. "This *has* been a definite improvement since the bedroom scene." I offered.

He looked apologetic again. "True. I wouldn't have imagined that's how we would have spent the first time you and I were in my room together."

"It's ok. The whole rescue and avenging my honor thing was flattering."

Just as I began leaning into the seat he pulled me toward him by tugging my neck gently in his direction. He brought his face to mine slowly and deliberately. I was taking pleasure in our proximity when he touched his lips softly to my face. His lips moved across my cheek and a rush of desire flew through my body as he just

43

barely kissed the corner of my mouth. It was so light I wondered if it was my imagination. He let go and I fumbled into my seat and buckled.

He was driving us back the way we had came when the significance of him leaving his own party dawned on me.

"Are you worried your house will be in shambles when we return?" I would have been terrified to leave my parents house with a bunch of idiots unsupervised. I was hoping for his sake that there hadn't been a problem while we were gone.

"If there are police cars outside when we get there I am just going to keep on driving." He said lightly. He didn't seem worried at all.

"So what am I supposed to do-tuck and roll out of the car?"

"Wow. You want to get away from me so bad you would flee a moving car?"

"No. But I do have a curfew. Not everyone's parents are out of town." I explained.

"Hmm. That's a shame." He looked over at me and I had to mash my lips together so I didn't squeal with excitement.

We turned onto his street and the majority of the cars were gone. The exterior of the house appeared benign and I hoped the inside would mimic it for Robert's sake. He parked in the driveway and walked me out to my car.

I got to the driver's side door and turned around to say goodnight. He must have been walking practically on my heels because his body was inches from mine. It was the second time tonight that we had stood this close and it was thrilling. My voice caught in my throat and I just stood before him smiling like an idiot.

"Be careful. Don't talk on your cell phone while you are driving. So many teenagers do that and it is a dangerous habit." He said it seriously but smiling at the same time.

"Are you channeling my mom? She said the same thing when I left the house." Would he ever stop harassing me? Sometimes I felt like he thought of me like a little sister. That would really suck.

It was 9 PM and I had been shackled to the phone for almost 24 hours now hoping Robert would call. I had done my best to avoid Jen and Jackie's attempts to reach me all day not sure what I should say about last night. I didn't know if we were keeping it a secret that he and I had hung out solo or not.

They were going to see a matinee, but I declined for fear he would call during the movie. It kind of ticked me off now because he hadn't called and I felt kind of pathetic waiting around.

I had been stuck inside with my parents all day. My new driver's license was beckoning to me from my wallet but I had nowhere to drive to. The only people wanting to make plans were the ones I was trying to avoid. And the one person I wanted to see wasn't calling.

At 10 o'clock when I had finally given up all hope the phone rang. I crossed my fingers before I looked at the screen. It was Robert. In my excitement I fumbled trying to hit the send button to receive the call.

"Hey, Robert." I said completely failing at hiding my excitement.

"Were you waiting for me to call?"

Damn him. Why did he always have to play with me? "I was just worried you might have gotten in trouble for the party. That's all."

"Nope. No trouble. I did have to clean the entire house by myself though."

"Your cousin didn't help?" I asked.

"No. He is still pretty pissed that I punched him and all. Remember?"

"Oh. Sorry."

"Don't be. Cleaning the house and punching him was definitely worth it in the long run." He said.

I was hoping he was alluding to the time he and I had spent together but he didn't actually say. Maybe he just meant he was glad he had thrown the party. Now that we had been apart all day I wondered if what I had felt last night was merely my imagination toying with me.

# Gift

Classes were going well. Actually I was impressed with how I had been able to master the curriculum so far. Truthfully I had to credit Robert and my relationship for that. Instead of passing notes and being distracted by each other's presence, I found we were challenging one another. We kept each other on our toes, poised for the next comeback, raced to answer questions posed by our teachers, and compared grades for bragging rights. The other students seemed happy to relinquish answering questions while absorbing the relationship between us. It was obvious to those of them who had all the same classes as us that we were constantly playing with each other. They took notice but didn't care. Our mutual friends weren't in class with us and were little aware of our connection.

We talked every night. I don't know what we filled the

phone line, with but it was a constant barrage that I anticipated every night as the clock inched towards nine.

We made a peculiar coupling-him always appearing to have stepped out of a Polo ad and I covered in eccentric outfits topped off with bizarre hair. Our shells were different in so many ways, but our personalities seemed perfect complements. I suppose our budding relationship was out of the ordinary but I had stopped examining it. Instead I just enjoyed it. We never verbally agreed to keep the night of the party a secret; it just ended up that way. That was fine. It meant fewer questions from Jen and Jackie.

A few weeks later we were all at the lunch table, it was a nondescript day in mid-October. We were engaged in separate conversations with friends but seemed electrically aware of one another. Jen and I were formulating costume plans for the masquerade ball in two weeks and were not coming up with any good ideas. Not surprisingly, she had been invited by an adoring senior. Troy was bartering Jackie for her pretzel rod in exchange for something from the lunch sack his mom had packed.

From the corner of my eye I watched Robert abruptly reach for his shoulder bag and produce a decently wrapped package. My interest was instantly piqued, but I didn't comment. I just watched him. Then he passed it to me across the table. Now everyone's attention was drawn to our interaction.

I reached for it with confusion saturating my face. We

usually kept a low profile when in plain view of our friends. We didn't really talk about our relationship. Not to say we were an item but our friendship was definitely significant. The secrecy our connection was enveloped in seemed to have been a silent agreement between us. He was changing the rules right in front of everyone.

I must have paused for a longer than acceptable time because Jen was eyeing me accusingly and harshly nudged the arm I was holding the package with. I opened it, peeked in, and laughed out loud.

I held my arm up high displaying the wide bands of red and black lining the knee high soccer socks hanging from my fingers to the table.

"Wow, sweaty soccer socks." I beamed at him and thought I caught a brief look of pain cross his face. Did he drop his cool façade for a moment? I locked eyes with him as the smile was returning to his face and offered an earnest "Thank you."

That's when I remembered that everyone else at the table had been scrutinizing our interaction. I scanned their faces and saw confusion, disbelief, and even a couple open mouths. I don't think it was the platonic words that had passed between us drawing their attention. It was more the connection that was practically palpable when we interacted with each other. I hadn't realized that the attraction would be obvious to anyone other than myself. Apparently I had been mistaken.

Robert appeared amused by the table's collective reaction

and ignored the onlookers focusing on me. "I was sure you could incorporate them into one of your outfits."

"I am considering a couple in my brain as we speak." I said.

He chuckled.

What had just happened? My heart was pounding in my chest and I was sure the thumping was audible to everyone within a 5 foot radius. They all melded back into their own conversations as I began studying the smashed bun on my hot ham and cheese sandwich while marveling in my head at the implications this last scene had.

One: He had given me a gift. Two: It was a thoughtful, personal gift. Not some generic card, candy, or flowers. Third: He had presented it to me in the middle of lunch period, at a table packed with our friends. I stole a glance at him beneath my eyelashes. He was discussing something with a friend and he held his frame in a relaxed sort of way. His presence made me want to smile. Not so much because I was drawn to his manicured pleasing looks but more because of his comforting manner. He was one of those rare people that can calm a room when he enters. He had a gentle happiness that emanated from his form. It wasn't something he tried to do; it was effortless, a natural part of who he was. I must have been doing some serious daydreaming because Jen was pinching me so I would walk with her to our next class.

Robert's never in a hurry, was continuing a conversation with a friend and smiled at me as I stood up. Instinctively I smiled back, not just a polite return smile but a beaming from ear to ear smile. It was like a reflex or something.  I wondered if he was aware of the power he had on my emotions?  It was as though his hands were controlling my face and heart with strings like a puppeteer.

She pinched me again disrupting my continued study of our nuances once again and we turned together walking away.  I felt like I was going to be interrogated.  Jackie and Jen both flanked me as we walked out of the cafeteria.

"What's up with the socks?" Jen asked.

"I don't know.  I guess he thought I would like them."

"Are you two going out?" Jackie questioned.

"I don't know." I answered honestly.

"Do you want to?" Jackie quizzed me.

"Yes," was my simple answer and I released all my inhibitions.  I hadn't realized how much that answer meant to me until I said it out loud.  It was freeing and the smile on my face somehow managed to get wider.

"I didn't know you thought he was cute." Jen said this in a confused way.  Not confused because she didn't know but that he was my object of affection.

"I do." It was that simple.  She arched her eyebrows with surprise at my directness and they smiled at one another.  They didn't see him the way I did.  He was not the most popular.  He was not captain of the football team or the life of the party.  Girls were not constantly trying to win his affection.  Like Jen had before, they flirted but they pursued bigger fish.  Their loss was my gain.  At least I hoped.

Our group made the announcement after the lunch table incident that we were an item without consulting us. Robert and I didn't protest, deny, or confirm the rumor. He accompanied me in the hallway to all our classes for the remainder of the week. People took notice of us. Whereas before he had a calm relaxed aura about him, now together we projected cheerfulness. The invisible connection the lunch table had sensed was now in plain view for everyone to watch. We held hands, teased, and whispered as we practically bounded down the halls. Life was great.

"What are you doing tonight?" I asked. It was Friday night, date night in high school. I was anticipating being with him, but I didn't know if I should assume that or not. We hadn't discussed it at all and classes were almost over for the day.

"I don't know. What am I doing?" He returned the question.

"Oh, its like that, huh?" I was thrilled. So he was obviously planning to be with me as much as I was planning to be with him. His toying grin was giving me goose bumps.

I smiled at him, pondering ideas for later tonight and marveled at my luck. His effect on me was almost comical in its potency.

"Ok, let me think about it. You want to meet at my house around 6:00?" I offered.

"Works for me."


I was getting ready for our date and sheer joy was coursing through every bit of me. It was invigorating, I was bounding out of the bathroom when my mom took notice. She eyed me warily with a grin on her face like I must be going crazy. I made a silly face and waved as I crossed into my room. It was one of those days where everything you try on looks great so it took me no time at all to get ready. I wore the red and black socks he had given me pulled past my knees where they met my black shorts and a fitted grey sweatshirt. Lots of girls would stand in the mirror for extended periods of time trying to look like a subdued version of a hot model but that wasn't me. I wouldn't be caught dead dressed up in a tight shirt, jeans, and heels with my hair perfectly placed on my head. I suppose there is nothing wrong with that, it just wasn't me. I would undoubtedly feel awkward and uncomfortable the whole evening.

I think I was daydreaming about Robert again when I heard the doorbell. I popped out of my stupor and was racing down the hall toward the stairs. I wanted to be the one that answered the door.

Apparently my mom had the same plan. I was barely out of my room when I heard her greeting; she must have been standing directly behind the door poised to answer it. I think she was desperately curious to find out who/what had me so keyed up.

My mom was cordial with Robert, the color of his skin was no more of consequence to her than it was to me. He was making polite conversation with her as I approached. He was wearing his wardrobe staple-the neatly ironed Polo shirt. Tonight it was white and was a beautiful contrast to the chocolate of his skin. He had paired it with khaki cargo pants and retro sneakers. I steadied myself after absorbing him.

I promised to call my mom later and swore to be home in time for curfew. With that she released us and we both took a deep breath as the door closed behind us and we stood side by side on the porch.

"Ready?" I asked.

"I don't know. I feel as though I am being taken hostage. I have no idea what our plans are."

"Are you scared?" I teased

"Terrified." This almost made me laugh out loud because his words were in such stark contrast to his relaxed demeanor.

"Don't worry. There are no blindfolds or duct tape in my bag. I thought we could go get ice cream. Does that sound ok?" We were almost at my car.

"Sounds perfect." He reached ahead and opened the door for me. I was sure that he was too good to be true.

I gave him a quizzical look.

"What?" He asked innocently.

"You always do that for people?"

"Yes. My dad really appreciates the gesture when I do it for him." he said sarcastically.

"You know what I mean." I pressed

"My mom raised me to open doors for the woman I was trying to impress."

"You are trying to impress me?"

"Only if it's working."

Seriously, he just gets better and better. Every layer I peel away from him sweetens the pot. On the surface was his screamingly good looks. Then his humor/sarcasm that complemented mine so well. His intelligence challenged me in an irritating way occasionally but usually I enjoyed every minute. Now he adds to that extreme politeness-it was disarming.

I drove us downtown, silently praying that I would not stall out with him in the seat next to me and that I wouldn't have to parallel park. Thankfully, I didn't stall out but the street was full and the couple open spots were for parallel parking. *Shit.*

Robert must have noticed the deer in the headlights look on my face because I heard a muffled chuckle from his seat. *Great.* Of course he would want to harass me about this.

"This is so funny, right?" I turned to him. I was annoyed. "If you are so fearless about parallel parking….be my guest." I parked the car in the middle of the street and opened his door where he was still sitting. "Come on. You're up." I motioned to the steering wheel.

He laughed again. Everything was so damn funny to him. He would not let the car behind us rush him and he waited for me to get in so he could close my door. He was incredible. I smiled despite my annoyance, loving that he didn't care what other people thought when it came to attending to me.

He parked at the spot I had angled the car for and had some amusing difficulty. We both laughed as the cars behind us lined up further back as he pulled out and readjusted the car for the second time.

I should probably explain that downtown Lewes, consists of one short main street with tourist shops lining both sides. Picture Mayberry from Andy Griffith and you are really close to what 2nd street looks like in reality. There was a mix of antique stores, clothing, jewelry, and coffee shops. There had been a hardware store for the longest time, but its space was now occupied by a unique toy shop. It was a rare sort where not everything was made of plastic or plastered in obnoxious TV characters.

Downtown was not a hot Friday night hang out spot, and the majority of couples we crossed paths with were over 40. We walked hand in hand down one side of the street looking in the windows and poking fun at the mannequins as we made our way to the ice cream store at the end. When we stepped into the shop, the sweet smell coated my nostrils and I clapped my hands excitedly. I swear I got more and more toddler-esque every minute I was around him.

I hadn't eaten much dinner and was studying the menu when the worker cleared his throat getting my attention.

"Hi...uh...I'll have chocolate ice cream, medium in a cup with double sprinkles, please."

"Do you want rainbow sprinkles or chocolate?" The attendant asked.

"Definitely rainbow sprinkles." I heard Robert chuckle softly behind me and I wheeled around "What!" I pretended to be offended.

He shook his head indulgently "I didn't think anyone ordered rainbow sprinkles outside of grade school." He joked.

"People just don't know what they are missing."

He was thoughtful for a moment. "I'll take the same as her please."

He carried our full dishes out to the benches that lined the front of the shop. We sat so close that our legs touched. The contact was incredibly distracting and I found myself thinking harder than necessary each time he or I shifted. I tried to suppress some of my excitement. It couldn't be normal to be so consumed by such an innocent position. Nevertheless my mind was intensely aware at the point where his leg converged with mine.

He was staring at me. I looked up and he took a big spoonful of ice cream coated with sprinkles.

"Oh my god. This is sooo good. Amazing really!" He exaggerated his words. I rolled my eyes.

"You know you like it." I pressed playfully.

We had held hands and nudged each other throughout our date but we hadn't kissed and this fact was in in the forefront of my mind as he drove us back to my house. I was nervous in my own car. Not uncomfortable nerves from it being just the two of us but because I was anticipating how he would seal the end of our date. It was the nervousness that results from wanting something so badly and also fearful you might get it. I sat still in my seat wondering if it would look like I ate a box of crayons from the rainbow sprinkles if he went to kiss me. I glided my tongue across my teeth inconspicuously hoping to dissolve any traitor sprinkles that might conspire to embarrass me.

He pulled into the driveway a few minutes before curfew. He walked me to the porch, our steps were hesitant and we lingered as we reached the door.

I looked up at him, and paused. "Kiss me" was practically a neon blinking sign on my forehead. My body language was screaming it…leaning into him, staring into his eyes, and my fingers playfully intertwining with his at waist level. It felt like the whole date had been culminating for this exact moment.

He smirked ever so gently and released one of his hands from mine; lifting it to shoulder level, he skimmed it down my arm. He tipped forward and started enveloping my upper lip with a slow, gentle peck. Then he drew his hand up my back and grasped my neck tenderly. I was moving my hands to his hips so I could better brace myself for what was surely to be the most amazing kiss ever shared between two people when my cell phone ring sliced through the air ruining the moment for all eternity.

*Damn it*! I silently berated myself.

It probably wouldn't have had such a sobering effect but the ring tone when my mom calls is her angrily screaming my name. I recorded it one day when she was pissed at me for something. It had always been funny until this very moment.

I looked up at him embarrassed, but he was smiling and I smiled too. I hit silence on my phone and retreated through the door before my mom threw it open and yanked me across the threshold by my arm.

As anticlimactic as our first kiss was it made official so much of our relationship. We were going out. We knew without question that Friday nights would be partaken by us together but more telling was that all our friends knew this too. Questions posed to us individually were always set in the plural tense ; "What are you guys doing tonight?" We spent every minute together possible, time which was facilitated by our shared classes.

I loved talking to him. I loved sitting quietly with him. I loved thinking about him. Our phone conversations were a nightly ritual. When I was apart from him, his smooth boyish face, the picture of it filled my head. I was practically drowning in my devotion to him. I let myself get lost in him, in us. Why not? We were young and invincible.

## Snow

It was 7 a.m. on an icy day in early December; I was sure the sane student body remained in a deep slumber because it was a snow day. I on the other hand was full of energy. Robert and I were positive the snow would keep school buses firmly parked so we had already made plans for today.

After two failed attempts I gave up on trying to look cute in snow gear and went for over-the-top silly instead. I mismatched everything possible, even wearing mismatched boots and gloves. There wasn't going to be much kissing and caressing with all this outerwear, so I was hoping to get a laugh out of him at least.

I saw him park his car through the living room window where I was staked out. I bounded through the door and ran to him full speed leaping at the end and forcing him backward into the snow. I rearranged myself so I was chin to chin with him.

"Hey!"

"How much coffee have you had this morning?" He asked alarmed.

"None."

"Is it drugs?" He feigned worry.

"Ha, Ha" I said slowly.

"I should talk to your mom about having an intervention."

"It's your fault that I am all crazy like this. Maybe I should give you up cold turkey?" I said.

"Sorry, that's not an option." Even though he was beneath me he managed to get up first so he could lift me onto my feet.

Robert drove my car to a park near his house. After the parallel parking incident there had been an unspoken contract that he was the responsible driving party.

There were big drifts of snow from the plows just as he had predicted, and he grabbed the plastic forms he talked excitedly about last night. We set to work packing the snow into the hollow forms and making blocks of ice. It was a painstaking process but gradually the fruits of our labor began to take shape. We were making an igloo literally brick by brick. By noon we were more than halfway done but were going to need some refueling before we could finish. The four hours of manual labor had dampened my earlier surge of energy.

"Shall we break for lunch?" He was pounding a brick at the back of the igloo. "I can make sandwiches at my house."

"As long as there's a bathroom, I don't care where we eat." I answered. I hadn't been to his house since the party and was kind of excited. It wasn't that I didn't feel welcome, he just always came to me.

I hovered over the cup of hot tomato soup he had heated for me trying to thaw myself. He leaned across the table and affectionately tucked my tousled hair behind my ear just as his mom was walking in. She mustn't have been expecting us to be there or maybe I was just the unwelcome addition because she halted her step immediately when her gaze rested on us. He obviously got his ironing addiction from his mom because the grey wool pants and fitted white shirt she was dressed in were unbelievably crisp. Her face mirrored the stiffness of her shirt.

I smiled innocently, not realizing how disturbed she was by the current scene playing out in her kitchen. I looked to Robert, and he was apologizing to me with pleading eyes. I creased my forehead; why did he look so worried?

He had met my parents many times, but I had only seen her in passing. This would be our first formal introduction, and it didn't seem to be starting off to well.

"Robert, what is going on?" Stern was not even the word for the seething way she spoke, and looked for that matter. She was eyeing me.

"Well, Mother, I am fixing a lunch of grilled cheese and tomato soup. Would you like some?" Somehow his formal words came off disrespectful.

"No."

"Suit yourself." He was almost taunting her now. I could tell there was a level of silent dialogue happening before my eyes, but I was completely missing it.

"Robert, I would like to speak to you. In private." She walked out of the room.

"I'll be right back." He said.

I was thinking this can't be good but was at a loss for what was happening. I couldn't hear what they were saying. All I caught was the angry tone passing between them. Then Robert got louder, and I could make out every determined word that tumbled from his mouth.

"Well, I am sorry you feel that way Mother, but Sophia and I will not yield to your prejudiced and offensive ideals. Didn't you know racism is passé? This is not some transient relationship. I realize you are disappointed it has lasted this long, but know this, our commitment will endure your backwards beliefs, future ordeals, and whatever else comes along." With that he stormed back into the kitchen and wrapped up our sandwiches, pulled me securely by the arm from where I sat stunned and we left.

He opened the car door and passed our wrapped lunch to me after I was in the seat. He angrily opened his own door, threw himself into the seat and slammed the shift into first gear. We were turning the corner when he turned his head, but not his eyes, toward me and said "I am so sorry."

I didn't know what to say. I was ashamed at my skin color for the first time in my life. If she hadn't liked my weird hair or crazy outfits I could change them, but this was something I could not fix. She didn't think I was good enough for her son. I was broken hearted. I was speechless. And then I was angry. I was boiling inside and then the flood gates opened.

"Why did you bring me there? Why would you flaunt me to her when she so obviously hates me? You knew how she felt and you sacrificed me to piss her off." I was screaming in the little car and it was ear piercing. Tears were streaming down my face. My words were flying jumbled out of my mouth. I was livid with him. "That is the most cold hearted thing anyone has ever done to me. I feel dirty. Like I did something wrong."

He listened, never protesting. How could he do this to me? Allow me to feel so embarrassed and ashamed. Then I saw where we were; at the park. "TAKE ME HOME! I don't want to be anywhere near you." I sobbed loudly into my hands, hoping that every choke and sniffle tore through his heart the way his mother's eyes had cut through mine. When I felt the car slow and rock back slightly, I heaved the door open and slammed it shut with every ounce of strength I had.

I collected myself enough to walk into the house, gather clean clothes, and undress. When I stepped into the steaming shower, I let every bit of my soul cry out with the pain they had caused me. When I felt that there were no tears left to cry, I just stood beneath the water, numb. I methodically dried myself, got dressed, and curled up on my bed, refusing to let all the stabbing questions enter. I didn't want to think about what the implications would be if his mom didn't want us to be together. I must have been exhausted from the emotional drama because I fell asleep and woke later in the pitch black of my room. It was empty and the silence was eerie. I hadn't wanted to be alone with my thoughts earlier, and now I was, to the extreme. It was just me.

I looked around my darkened room. I had a nice, comfortable home. I kept my room decent, not impeccable…I was a teenager. I looked into the darkened room and saw my bronze award from the fifth grade science fair. I had done a presentation on geysers. Somewhere in the black of my room was a picture of my dad and I dressed up for a Christmas Eve service. I was typical. I respected my parents the majority of the time. I had good school attendance. I was in all the advanced courses.

I was white. The ache in my chest began to open again. I was distracted by a glow that appeared to be floating over by my closet door. Then I recognized it as the light from my cell phone resting on my dresser. I hadn't checked it since I had stormed in the house earlier. Which seemed like so long ago. I picked myself up and fumbled across my room trying not to break my neck on the books and other miscellaneous obstacles lying strewn across the floor. I rubbed my eyes and opened the phone with my thumb.

I wanted it to be him so badly. Why was it that even though he was the source of my pain he was the only one that I yearned for? I wanted to push him away, but I wanted him to be relentless about chasing after me. I wanted to be alone, but I wanted him with me. I wanted him to hold me and tell me everything would be ok, that he would make everything ok. I wanted to scream, kick, and cry…in his arms.

There were ten missed calls. Robert had called me every hour on the hour since I had left him. His last attempt to reach me was a text message. I pressed read hesitantly. Dying to know what it said but worried as well.

*The image of you hurting because of this…it's defeating me. I am desperate for you.*

His words were raw. He was always candid and open with me but this was deeper. Earlier when he sat in the car so cold and quiet, I wanted him to hurt. I wanted to hurt *him* the way I was hurting. I wanted to crash through his stone calm and make him cry. But now, I just wanted to console him. I made myself release the phone from my clutched fingers. I would not forgive so easily, no matter how intensely my soul begged me to. Not yet.

My feet thudded as I found my way back to my bed. I didn't even have the mind to crawl under the covers. I curled myself up, hugging my knees, and lay atop my down comforter. It fluffed up and enveloped me.

Later, there was knocking at my bedroom door and dull light streamed between the curtain panels. I thought about throwing something at it in response but there wasn't anything in my hand, so I just breathed "Go Away."

"Robert is downstairs" My mom lamented. "He doesn't look

good."

I had held myself up in my room since yesterday afternoon and no one had knocked, left dinner outside the door, or made sure I hadn't slit my wrists but now Mom was concerned because Robert "didn't look good". What the hell!

I dragged myself off the bed. I needed to get up and pee anyway. I didn't look at my mom and just headed toward the bathroom.

"I'll tell him you're coming down." Gee, thanks mom; your gonna be all helpful now I guess.

He wasn't in the living room, so I assumed he was on the porch. I stepped out into the frigid air. He had been standing with his back to the door and appeared to be concentrating hard, looking skyward. It was the first time that the pit of my stomach reacted in an anguished way when I took in his form. Was it yesterday that I was bounding out the door to tackle him in the snow? We felt a million miles apart now, even though he was within arms reach.

He turned and gave me an apprehensive smile. He had balled up my coat to shield it from the cold, and now he unraveled it and helped me put it on. I guess I left it yesterday when I blew out of his car. He zipped it for me like I was a toddler, and I looked up to his face. I am not sure if I was forcing myself, to look or letting myself but when I did his sorrowful gaze washed over me.

"I am so sorry." He was holding back tears. He was waiting for me to let him back in; to forgive him.

"I know."

He locked his arms around me and we clung to each other for a long time. Still holding me he explained, "I had no idea she would react like that. I knew she wasn't happy about our being a couple, but I had thought it would pass. I had been open with her, telling her over and over how important you were to me. I thought if she could just see us together she would see the undeniable connection. I never meant to hurt you. I hate that…"

I shook my head back and forth interrupting him. I had heard enough. "It's ok. It'll work out somehow."

"Can I take you somewhere? Show you something?"

"Now?" I was barely awake.

"Yes. Now." He said definitively and cupped my hand, leading me down the steps.

There was hot coffee waiting for me in the passenger seat cup holder. He new my weaknesses so well. I smirked and reached for it.

He drove carefully across the packed snow that covered the streets. His pace was unhurried, and I enjoyed looking at how the white blanket made everything so different. He pulled into the same spot as yesterday at the park. I walked around to the hood of the car where he was and shrugged at him.

"I don't really feel like manual labor today." Alluding to my disinterest in making ice bricks.

"Don't worry, I think you have expended enough of your energy in the last twenty-four hours."

We had been walking forward and now I saw that the igloo

we had started was complete and picturesque. It had been dusted with snow that morning and appeared so authentic, like we could be on a different continent. Its location in the park with trees in the background looked more like a fairytale.

"This is amazing. You did this?"

"Concentrating on building this was better than torturing myself with images of you hating me."

I walked ahead of him. Exploring the perimeter. I bent my head down to creep through the opening and he followed me. The most impressive part of the igloo was that the interior was decently warm. We sat next to each other with our backs leaning on the ice wall.

He turned his face to mine. "Your face yesterday…looking at me. When you thought that I had willingly let you be hurt…" He tightened his jaw and continued "I would never have taken you near my mom if I thought she would react like that. I wouldn't purposefully let someone hurt you. I would never do that." He paused again. "I will do everything in my power to never have that look cross your face again. I want to protect you, and care for you."

He put his hands on either side of my face fixing our eyes directly on each others "I love you."

I let his words settle through me. It wasn't bittersweet. His love was not tainted or touched by the trial we had just experienced. His words completely replaced the hurt, shame, and anger I had felt so powerfully before. My face broke out into one of those ridiculously huge grins and I instinctively brought my lips onto his for the first time.  Usually I let him initiate our make out sessions but my body was yearning for him to touch and hold me in a desperate way.  He obliged by molding our bodies together.  I realized that though we were not invincible, our connection would only strengthen with each trial we overcame.  Regardless of time, tears, and tests we would persevere.

The kiss and embrace we had just shared felt momentous.  I wasn't concentrating on anything except his arms tightly enclosing me when his cool voice broke through the silence.

"I am feeling sort of rejected over here.  I mean don't feel any pressure to say it because I did…but…"  He was obviously going to continue babbling in this kidding manner, and it was starting to interrupt my utter enjoyment of his hold so I reciprocated his affection with words instead of demonstration.

"I love you"

He smiled; satisfied.


A week later we were sitting on my bed studying for the English final, a comprehensive exam on Jane Eyre.  The once loathed, worn book containing the love story between the books namesake and Mr. Rochester lay open in my hands.  I had initially regarded the assignment as punishment but ended up falling in love with the heroine.  She was alone in the world, but refused to tame her loose tongue, to ease her existence.  I was thrilled by her brazen comments and sometimes laughed aloud at her surprising tenacity.

I was rereading a favorite passage to myself: *the sarcasm that repelled, the harshness that had startled me once, were only keen condiments in a choice dish.* She was referencing her secret love and how she interpreted his negative elements as necessary components now.

Robert's voice cut int my thoughts. "My mom is making me go to Georgia for Christmas vacation."

My head snapped in his direction. "Huh?"

"My mom is forcing me to go to Georgia as soon as finals are complete and stay the entire winter break at my Uncle's house. Her and Dad are going to come down for a few days before and after Christmas."

"How long have you known this?" I asked accusingly.

"I knew she was going to make us all spend Christmas there but she just told me last night at dinner that I was sentenced to the entire break. I am really sorry. I already tried protesting but she bought the ticket on Monday."

I paused absorbing it all. "She wants us apart?" I spoke the words as the realization came to my mind.

"Yes. She is so deluded. She's clinging to a ridiculous hope that keeping us apart for three weeks is going to in someway break us up."

There was a sting somewhere in my subconscious that I did not acknowledge. I laughed instead. "She's gonna be so pissed when she figures out she's wrong."

## Leaving

We were right on the verge of finals. I felt like my brain could not possibly retain any more information. Seriously, who cares about solving the value of x. Isn't that what calculators are for? Jen and Jackie were starting to harass me because if I wasn't studying with Robert; we were hanging out doing something else or nothing else but undoubtedly doing it together. We had checked out books at the library, went swinging on the elementary school playground, and one rainy Saturday we had covered a wall in my bedroom with chalkboard paint.

Quite early in our relationship Robert had become a regular fixture at our nightly dinners. My mom had really taken a liking to him, and I sometimes teased that she might be my toughest competition. She was charmed by his dress, manners, and general soothing air. I really couldn't hold that against her though because they topped my list too; but I felt like I could add a hundred more. I loved his smile, so genuine. I loved that he religiously shaved so that his head and face were always milky smooth. I loved tracing the muscle that ribbed out on his bicep. I loved the way he looked at me adoringly. I loved the way without trying he stirred my emotions. There were less cheesy romantic reasons that I found him absolutely irresistible also. He thought to bring me coffee at random times. His feet were inordinately big but he carried them easily. His calm confidence could at times be construed as cocky, but he was just too damn polite for that. He was relentlessly sarcastic. When he spoke there was an undercurrent of slight teasing with whomever he was talking with, but so often I was the only one able to pick it up. It was like he was talking to them outwardly, but having a silent conversation underneath simply to amuse me.

We hadn't talked about him going away for Christmas. I don't think we were purposely ignoring it; there was just a lot going on, and why dwell on something we had no control over. Christmas vacation had flown by too fast every other year, and I am sure that would be the case this year.

As for finals, I figured it would be the first and only time in my life when I would not want them to end. I was dreading the weeks we would be apart. At the same time I was looking forward to the disappointment Mrs. Warren would feel when she saw her plan fail. We finished our last final Thursday afternoon. As I colored in the bubble for the last question, my stomach twisted, and I was sure it had nothing to do with the test. The fact that finals were over and Robert would be leaving in the morning had been making my hand tremor slightly for the last fifteen questions. I handed my test to the teacher and walked back to my desk. Robert had already finished and had my backpack strapped to him along with his own. I almost cried right there in class.

We drove to my house and hung out in my room. Since the semester was officially over, I decided all the study notes, quotes, questions, and equations that had accumulated during our study sessions could be erased from the chalkboard wall we had painted. Robert and I worked side by side trying not to douse the carpet with dusty water as we washed the wall. There were a few notes at the very top he had written while standing on a stool, and we couldn't reach them. I balled up my wet rag and with a little jump threw it at the letters hoping to erase a few at a time. It did a decent job, but Robert got sprayed with the dirty water when it ricocheted off the wall. He turned to me and I had to laugh because his perfectly ironed shirt was now splattered with chalky droplets.

A split second later I was hit with a soaking wet rag right in my mid section. I was shocked that he had gone so far. Usually he was so conscientious about being neat in my parents house. I put my hand in the bucket and splashed water up at him with my cupped hand. He shielded himself with his right arm and then tackled me as I reached in for another handful to toss. We wrestled for a brief moment before he brought me down on my back and pinned my wrists to the carpet with his hands. We stared at each other with mischievous grins and heaving chests.

"That wasn't nice." I said still breathing hard.

"You started it." He teased.

"Either way I thought you had better manners than to tackle a girl." He was still holding me down by my wrists, but I wasn't fighting him.

"I thought you liked when I tackled you?" He responded. He bent his head down and kissed me. Kissing him always made me feel incredible and we didn't stop for awhile, knowing there wouldn't be too many more. He relinquished my wrists, and we groped at each other. I felt like I needed to touch every part of him so I could remember every inch while he was gone.

Miraculously he had convinced his mom to let me drive him to the airport. She dropped him off the morning after finals at 6:30 a.m.. He loaded his bags into my car and came right into the house. I was ready and waiting, enjoying my first cup of coffee at the dining room table. He took in my outfit grey comfy pants, a purple striped long sleeve shirt that I overlaid with his yellow junior high soccer team tee, and moccasin slippers.

"What!" I said defensively. He was rarely fazed by my uncoordinated colors.

"You need shoes. It's winter." He was as bad as my mom, who was still religiously throwing a coat at me in the morning that I was forever hanging back up.

"I'm going to be in the car all day. I want to be comfortable." I whined.

"I'm going to get you a pair of sneakers. You are at least

75

bringing a pair."

Fine, whatever; I thought to myself. As long as he didn't expect me to go get them. I would just gulp down the rest of my cup before we had to leave. His mom would have a conniption if he missed his flight. He darted up the stairs and was coming back down as I put my mug in the dishwasher.

He drove, so I was tasked with navigating. This was a frightening thought because my sense of direction rivaled that of a drunk mouse. He was just turning off our road, fixing the mirrors, and adjusting his seat when...

"Your car was do for an oil change 9,000 miles ago!" He said alarmed. Was he worried we wouldn't make the two hour drive to the Baltimore airport?

"Its fine. I've gone longer than that before." I said off hand.

"It's really bad for your engine. Promise me you will get it changed over break."

"Promise." I held my hand up like I was taking an oath. He just shook his head as he so often does with me. I was flipping through the stations when one of my favorite songs came on. I cranked up the volume and started singing. Well, it was really more screaming than singing. My enthusiasm was infectious and Robert started singing at the top of his lungs too.

I took our picture in; young, ferociously happy, carefree, and thought how lucky we were to have found each other. Everything would be right in my world as long as he was included. Our eyes met and we smiled.

The airport coming into view was a sobering vision. The drive had gone entirely too fast and I was not ready to say goodbye. I grabbed my sneakers while he parked the car.

"I'd give you a piggyback, so you wouldn't have to wear those but I don't want you trying to hitch a ride on some stranger to get back to your car." He was trying to lighten the mood and I appreciated the attempt.

"You're such a gentleman," I kidded, but my heart wasn't in it. I couldn't pretend that we were just enjoying another day together with his departure looming right before us.

We walked hand in hand through the cold and into the airport. I stood by his side, quiet, as he steered us through all the necessary check-in points. We were approaching the security screening area and I knew I would not be allowed any further. My chest tightened, and I clutched his hand tighter. The tears were about to spill, and I didn't think I could hold them back for another second. Reality was overwhelming me, as I tried to hold myself together. He stopped walking just before the line and turned to face me.

I felt like it was all in slow motion. My throat was tight and my stomach knotted. I looked up to meet his eyes, to absorb every detail of his face and commit it to memory. I wanted to be able to draw it from my mind on demand whenever I needed him. His cheeks with a boyish roundness, his skin ever smooth, his eyes deep. He took in my pained face.

"You know what they say…distance makes the heart grow

fonder," he said lightly.

"Whoever said that should be shot," I choked out. My face suddenly twisted into a reddened, tear covered mess.

"Please don't cry. This is going to go by so fast." He hugged me. "Take care of yourself, ok…not too much coffee, don't put your buns in too tight; you'll give yourself a migraine. And get your oil changed."

"I'm going to miss you every freaking minute." I sniffled into his chest.

"Me too." Then he kissed me. A sweet simple romantic peck that spilled over with the intense emotions we were both experiencing.

We whispered I love you to each other, gave one last tight squeeze, and then we disconnected from each other. I wanted to watch him as he went through the line, until he walked out of view, but I didn't want to cry so openly before the other passengers.

I clenched my jaw, turned around and walked determinedly down the corridor, not looking back. I passed the front desk, stepped into the cold parking lot, fell into my seat, locked the door and released. I cried while music blared from the speakers; I was trying to drown out my sobs so I wouldn't have to hear the pain in them. It didn't take me that long to get it all out. It unleashed from me with such force that I didn't have to endure it for long. Exhausted, I put my key in the ignition and drove home, in silence. I didn't want to think or feel. I let the intricacies of driving distract my brain. I didn't want to consider the physical distance that was increasing between Robert and me as every second passed. I felt hollow and numb.

My mom's reaction to my appearance when I returned home conveyed that I wasn't holding myself together as well as I thought. She looked concerned, to put it mildly.

"Are you ok, honey? I'm sorry." She hugged me and patted the side of my face like a child. I just nodded my response into her chest.

"Jen called for you. She said she tried to call you on your cell phone but there was no answer. Why don't you call her?" She spoke gently and it made me appreciate that she wasn't trivializing my hurt or the situation.

"I will." Jen had been such a good friend. She wasn't jealous that I had spent the majority of my time with Robert over the last semester. She was glad to hang out and only teasingly harassed me about all the time he and I spent alone together. I couldn't ask for a more understanding friend.

I padded the stairs up to my room and threw myself on the bed. I should call her but the caffeine effects of this morning had worn off, and the fact that I woke up at 5:45 to get ready caught up with me, and I fell soundly asleep.

I woke up startled, and with drool on my pillow. Definite confirmation that I slept well. I lazily rolled over and saw it was noon! Robert should have well arrived by now and been able to call. I dug through my bag and found my cell phone.

It was on vibrate. No wonder I hadn't answered Jen's call

earlier. I should really disable that feature. There were 3 missed calls. Two were from Jen, then my heart leaped a little when I saw Robert had called me just ten minutes ago. Seeing his name spelled out on my phone generated the all too familiar giddy reaction he had on me. Apparently distance did not lessen the effect.

I immediately hit send, filling with butterflies anticipating his smooth voice coming through the phone to my ear. Not as fulfilling as physical presence but at least something.

His voice broke through the dead air, and I'm pretty sure I squealed audibly. "Hey, I called you." His greeting was bursting with enthusiasm.

"I know sorry. I fell asleep when I got home and just now woke up. How was your flight?" I was grinning and nervously flicking my tooth with my thumb nail.

"It was fine. Quick. We just got to my Uncle's, and I'm unpacking some stuff. My cousins are really excited to see me, but are already tired of hearing me ramble about you."

I giggled. "Well, try not to bore them to death with minutia."

"So are you just going to sleep for three weeks until I get home?"

"Yes; I'm hopeless, just rename me Anastasia."

"Huh?" He missed my reference.

"Sleeping Beauty. Jeez, you were so deprived as a child." I teased.

"Oh." He said as the reference dawned on him.

"No. Actually Jen called me so I was going to get up with

80

her I think."

"Good. Have Fun. I hate to think of you lying in your room and mourning me the entire time."

"Well, that's exactly what I expect of you." I instructed.

" I think my cousins would harm me if I never left this room, but I will hold out as long as I can. Oh, they're calling for me. I'll talk to you soon." He responded.

"You're such a sell out. You didn't even make it 24 hours hold up in you room."

"Ha-Ha. I love you." He concluded.

"I love you, too."

I called Jen next. It was good I had talked to Robert first because it yanked me out of the gloomy mood I had been in. She was going to the movies with a bunch of other kids from school, so we planned for her to pick me up early enough to grab a bite to eat first.

We were catching up on school, grades, and gossip over fries when she spotted Troy. She waved at him and he bee lined for our table, of course. Jen was looking as enticing as always with her blonder hair flowing below her shoulders, a tight pink v-neck tee, big silver hoop earrings, and a necklace that was just the right length to draw attention to her chest. Somebody else might look trashy but she never did. She always just looked well put together.

"Hey, Troy. How are you?" The smile that crossed her face was meant to tempt.

"Good." One word responses were common around Jen.

81

Guys could only formulate simple answers when their minds were so otherwise engaged.

"We're headed to the movies with Jackie, Valerie, Adam, and Dan. You want to come?"

"Sure." I almost felt sorry for him. It was like he was in a trance and might start to drool at any moment. I thought if I broke into his concentration he might be able to speak coherently again.

"Cool. We're going to Dead End at 6:00." I said. His eyes released when I spoke, and I think he saw me for the first time.

"Ok." Never mind he is hopeless.

"Have you heard from Robert?" He asked seeming to have found his bearings finally.

"Yea. His flight got in fine and he was unpacking a couple hours ago." I answered.

"Well, tell him I said Hi next time he calls."

"I will." We planned a spot to meet back up at the movies and he went back to his table where he was eating with his parents.

"Do you like him?" I questioned Jen.

"Who? Troy!" She was amused.

"Never mind. You just can't help your natural allure and the reaction it spurs in boys I guess." We laughed together. It was fun hanging out with her.


It was Tuesday and after 10 o'clock. I was staring at my cell phone willing it to ring. Robert had been reliably calling every night around this time to say goodnight but tonight he was with his cousin.

Robert told me earlier in the day that Chandra, Ricky's girlfriend, had broken up with him. I guess it really had Ricky upset, and Robert agreed to try and cheer him up.

I was staring at the massive countdown calendar I had drawn on the wall after Robert left. Each morning I would cross a huge X through the previous day and it gave me some consolation that another day was done. So far we had trudged through almost a full week, which left two weeks to go. We weren't even half way through. Time definitely was not going as fast as I had hoped, but I didn't tell Robert that. I didn't want him to worry, and I didn't want our conversations to be depressing, so we usually talked about other incidentals.

I repeatedly told myself that this situation was temporary and in twenty years we would probably laugh at how dire we had considered it. I propped my head up on the pillow, laid my phone on my stomach, and opened Jane Eyre.

What we once enjoyed and deeply loved,

Even for a short while, We can never lose.

For all that we deeply love becomes a part of us.

-Helen Keller

**Five Years Later**

## Reality

*beep,beep,beep*…the welcome sound that most people completely detest broke through another night of sleep. It was 5 a.m.; I could see the dawn starting to force itself through the window blinds Troy had shut last night before bed. Cold winter air was relentlessly forcing itself through my socked and slippered feet beneath the bed covers. I gave a long stretch and eased out of bed.

Troy was more than a sound sleeper, so I don't know why I bothered trying to be quiet as I changed into my favorite yoga pants and laced my sneakers. When I reached the driveway the sun was winning the morning battle, and the nighttime darkness had mostly receded. I am not much for warming up or stretching, so I set my music to loud and got lost as my feet hit the pavement. I could feel all the ties that bind me to a constant level of stress release as I turned onto the road. The repetitive motion was calming, and my mind enjoyed the quiet. It was a really good run, one when your body is churning out the necessary steps but without any conscious effort. My arms and legs were in complete unison as I found myself directly in front of the stop sign that marked my halfway point; I had to practically force myself to turn and head home. I would have loved to continue, but I had a lot to do today.

Before I permitted myself, my brain had begun cataloging the tasks for the day and planning my itinerary to the last detail. Of course they were already clearly written in my immaculate planner, ready to be crossed off as soon as they were complete.

I saw our house up ahead, a blue and white townhouse jutting out on the corner of our road. I walked into the kitchen passing through the garage where there appeared to be no organization, a clear sign this was not my domain. The kitchen on the other hand was kept neat and uncluttered and flowed into the dining room. The rooms were divided by a butcher block topped island complete with barstools. Troy and I started renting the two bedroom townhouse a few months back much to my mom's dismay. I didn't see the big deal. We were engaged to be married and sharing a place saved us money.

I started making coffee as I heard Troy's alarm sound for what must have been the tenth snooze because he was actually getting up this time. He popped his head out and garbled good morning as I took in his obvious sleepy face with signs of a pillow impression on one of his mashed thick brown eyebrows and creased on his cheek. The intoxicating smell of coffee began to permeate the kitchen and I started making Troy's sandwich. I slipped a little note in for him to call me later before I closed the lid. I perused my to do list for the day and just rolled my eyes. Shower first.

I heard Troy's heavy boots cross the kitchen floor, pause to pick up his lunch and coffee, and head out. I was towel drying when I read the note he had scribbled on the bathroom mirror-*Sophia I love you, have a good day*.

I was wearing my self enforced uniform of khaki pants with a sweater. At the private school where I had started teaching fifth grade in the fall students were required to wear uniforms, but teachers were not. It was just easier this way. It made my morning routine flow smoother always having a set idea of what I would wear. I drove to work in my well loved Mazda and mentally reviewed my teaching plan for the day.

I had graduated from college the spring before and was lucky to get a job at the only private school in southern Delaware. I was enjoying the students for the most part but the schedule was the most priceless piece of the pie. I worked Monday through Thursday from 7 a.m. until only 2 p.m.. Those seven hours were intense and a great deal of learning was expected of the students. Following classes students were required to attend two additional hours of extracurricular activities. On Fridays, students and teachers were off. This is how you knew these families were different from the average Wal-Mart shoppers. They had managed to completely reconfigure the school week so that they could travel more frequently or whatever it was they did.

I was working really hard to prove myself; I didn't want this job slipping through my fingers. That meant my lesson plans had to be perfect, students had to be excelling, and I needed to look how the parents expected their little Johnny's teacher to look. I was participating in student council as a faculty advisor and also an educational panel for spearheading improvements throughout the Eastern shore public school system. It was time consuming but I hoped it would help the administrators see my worth.

When I pulled into the parking lot it was still mostly vacant. I was used to that. I liked to be there early so I was well prepared when the students filed into class. I sat at my desk and peered out my window, gulping my last sips of coffee while Mercedes, Lexus's, and BMW's rolled to the curb and kids covered in navy and khaki jumped out. The day ticked by uneventfully as we completed the math, reading, geography, and history work I had prepped. The students and I were equally as happy when the bell rang to dismiss them from school.

I crossed the parking lot to my car where it stood out like a sore thumb between the shiny SUV's and luxury cars everyone else drove. I adjusted myself in my seat and grabbed my planner. I crossed through SCHOOL and looked to my next task for the day: CHAIR COVERS.

## Planning

For some the idea of planning a wedding by themselves would seem daunting, but I reveled in the chaos of confirming orders and times with the caterers, florists, priest, cake decorator, and all the additional personnel who were hired to help my wedding vision become reality. I was like a conductor leading an orchestra. It was thrilling, controlling it all, and hand picking each piece of the puzzle to my liking. Seriously, I wish Troy and I could get married every year.

I wasn't into over-the-top affairs with silly ice sculptures or elaborate menus though. Centerpieces would be simple glass vases filled with a bouquet of wildflowers, similar to the one Troy surprised me with at school on our one year anniversary. Guests would be dining on spaghetti and meatballs because it is the no fail dinner he cooks for me on a semi-regular basis. A slide show was set to play showing brief clips of us as we grew up and through the five years we had dated. Five years. WOW. That is a long time but we started going out when we were in high school. Since that time we had been busy growing up as individuals and as a couple as we completed college, started careers, and moved back home to a nondescript town in Delaware.

Troy had taken a job with the local fire company following in his father's footsteps, and this explained another piece of our wedding, the ceremony and reception would take place at the fire hall. The fire company had been a big part of his childhood, and it would surely be a big part of our marriage as well. We have had some of our worst fights in relation to the fire company, so this was my way of embracing that part of him and committing to working through the difficulty it posed. People don't realize that when your father or husband is a fire fighter, so much of your life revolves around the company's needs.

"uh…yes I am *still* holding. Look, it's not that big of a deal. Cream or white chair covers…it doesn't make a difference to me as long as they all match."

"Oh, okay, Ms. Lake. In that case let me go ahead and put down cream because we are sure to have those available for you."

"Great." A phony smile pressed across my face even though I was in my kitchen at home staring fixedly at my coffee cup that was dangerously low for the length of this conversation. At least I got to cross something off my list. The remainder of the afternoon progressed in a similar manner as I hammered out final details of the wedding.

I heard the door knob rotating as I was crossing off one of the last items on my list.

Crap, was it that time already…I hadn't thought about, let alone started dinner. I stepped off the bar stool and stretched my arms wide as Troy walked in with the mail under one arm and his lunch box in the other.

"Hey, I didn't do anything for dinner. Been working on wedding details so I'm going to pop a pizza in, K."

"Well, if its cool, we got a new pump in today and Matt and I were gonna meet up and look it over tonight."

"Oh. That's okay I guess."

Truthfully, I was relieved on a level that I would not allow myself to comprehend. An hour later I slid into the tub and gripped my most recent issue of Newsweek as I situated my body. I was forcing myself to read an article that was part of a series concerning education in The States vs. China and India. Nothing like dry news to relax you in the tub.

It was hours later when I was sleeping that I was woken by Troy shuffling into the room and slinking into bed. I pretended to be sound asleep as I caught the typical smell of alcohol on his skin and breath. I squeezed my eyes tighter and forced myself to fall back to sleep as he searched for my hand beneath the covers and curled his fingers tenderly into mine.


On Saturday I woke again wrapped in Troy's embrace.

When he felt me shift he instinctively squeezed tighter. It was futile to think I could enjoy sleeping in past 8:30 am, and I finally surrendered to the morning person that was ingrained into my genetic makeup and headed toward the shower.

In the kitchen, Troy swallowed polite mouthfuls of coffee as I gulped mine, just trying not to scorch my tongue. My coffee addiction was pathetic, but there were worse things. The empty Saturday hours stretched long before us, and the rain pounding on the windows was making the couch beckon stronger by the minute. He proposed, movie day which was tempting but I had to clean the house first. It was my Saturday routine and I wouldn't be able to relax until the house was just so. I wiped, scrubbed, and mopped every inch of the house until all surfaces were silky smooth and all miscellaneous items were returned to designated places. Jackie liked to poke fun at this absurd need to have all aspects of my life in precise order and had teased on many an occasion that medication would be helpful. My retort had been: *Why would I take medication, I like it this way.* After I was satisfied that no one in the development could possibly have a cleaner house than mine, I plopped onto the couch.

Troy and I surveyed our respectable collection of movies and debated which one to start with. We equally enjoyed the action movies and the sappy romantic ones too. So the day was filled with a variety of our favorites and I was relieved that his stupid pager never went off calling him to the station. Its presence on the coffee table would not let me completely forget the possibility though.

Sometimes I felt like it was our omnipresent third wheel, but not for a night's date instead for our lifetime. I immediately felt like a selfish person when I regarded the fires he went to as a disruption to our life. Its like when you complain about a traffic jam and then find out that people died in the accident. You feel like a jerk.

We ate spaghetti for dinner. It was my favorite, singly because he prepared it for me. We crawled into bed together that night and it was the perfect ending to a relaxing and effortless day. Days like this made me feel wholly content.


On Monday, after work, I proudly muscled in all the bags of groceries in one trip. I was planning Hawaiian chicken and rice with grilled pineapples, so I left any groceries needed on the counter.

The voicemail on my phone buzzed. "Hey, honey…I just got a page so I'm going to respond. It's 4:15 now, not sure when we'll be done. Call you when I can. Love ya." Troy hung up.

That familiar hollow feeling creeped in. I suppose it was a mix of fear and annoyance, but it made me want to growl at the chicken. Oh, well. If I don't need to have dinner ready yet I'll have time for a run. I slipped into my well worn sneakers and felt the unease subsiding. By the time I reached the end of the driveway it was completely erased, and I was invigorated by the beautiful sunset before me. Of course on a day I had ample time for a long run my body wouldn't cooperate. My feet were trudging along and I just couldn't get the right rhythm. Figures. I cut the run short and headed home.

Troy wasn't there yet. Not that I was surprised but I was hoping for a message on the machine. Nothing. My cell phone was on the charger and there were no missed calls or messages on it either.

I wasn't much of a chef and rarely had the ambition to cook when it was just me so I quick fixed a turkey sandwich with leftovers and settled onto the couch in time for the six o'clock news. Crap, the news was depressing but I forced myself to watch imagining it was the mature thing to do. Like I was fulfilling some sort of adult duty. The silent phones next to me kept drawing my attention.

I couldn't help the terrible scenarios that crept into my mind. Troy caught in a building. Troy struck by falling debris. Troy crawling on an ash covered floor with flames shooting above him. It was torture. And then there were the less noble images. Troy drinking at the station. Troy playing cards with the guys. Troy swerving on the road. I couldn't get my mind to rest as the different scenes played relentlessly in my mind.

I kept checking the phones.

Finally I text him: *Hey, u ok?*

*Yup, I'm good. Be home soon.*

That didn't completely ease my mind, but I was able to narrow down the possibilities of where he was. He surely was not texting me from beneath a burning structure. Well, if he wasn't hurt then I was going to bed. I had wasted enough time worrying about his well-being for one night.

I woke up in the morning with Troy's fully clothed body invading my half of the bed. I reached over and turned my alarm clock off a minute before it was going to start its timed beeping. My morning routine was so repetitive. I made coffee, Troy's lunch, poured a cup, showered, and then dressed. I progressed through my morning tasks in a robotic manner.

I continued in this way concentrating on the tedium, not allowing myself to replay the episode of last evening. I was tired. Not because it was morning or due to the fact that the majority of my night had been filled with restless sleep clouded by worry over his whereabouts, but I was tired of Troy's persistent reckless behavior that continually forced me to consider disturbing scenarios. The images that were summoned to mind were always the same. I had replayed them so many times, and it appeared that each time I revisited them the impression left became more invasive. It was like harming a recently healed wound. Each occurrence caused the offended area to intrude further into my memory. It hurt.

"Troy, you shouldn't have been driving last night." I was upfront and firm when he walked into the kitchen. He would have preferred I ignore the incident but also knew that was not likely.

"It's fine. I'm fine. See." He exaggerated the comment by putting his arms out and turning his entire body around for display. "Don't worry." He approached me and encircled my frame with his arms. He looked at me with a sad puppy dog face. My features remained hard until he hugged me tight.

It had a cleansing effect. I let myself release the hurt and anger like so many times before, and I hugged him back. He moved his hands up and down my back trying to massage away the pain. There was no point in staying mad. The only one fazed here was me.

The day's leading up to our wedding were growing shorter and I was glad that I had planned ahead so well. The details were ironing out just as I had hoped and it appeared everything would turn out without a hitch. I was looking forward to the stillness and unhurried pace of the honeymoon that would follow.

All I had left to figure out was transportation to the airport. We weren't planning on driving ourselves because we were leaving directly from the reception. I pulled out the yellow pages and started with Atlas the first company listed under transportation. As I worked my way down the list providing the same trip details and asking the same questions about price, I picked up Troy's things around the house. It was an endless task. His boots were by the garage door, his breakfast dishes were in the sink, and his helmet was on the counter. He didn't usually bring it home and now he would have to use one of the extras at the station if needed today. Maybe when I finished with the transportation plans and some work I could bring it to him. I marinated the chicken I hadn't made last night with a Hawaiian sauce, covered it with plastic wrap, and put it back in the refrigerator.

"Look, the best deal I've been given so far is 45.50 for one way. If you would be willing to beat that price then I will make the reservations right now." I was getting tired of the wheeling and dealing. I just wanted to be off the phone.

"Let me check with a manager Ms. Lake."

It struck me that I wouldn't be Ms. Lake much longer, and my gaze zeroed in on the diamond on my left hand. It was such a pretty ring; I loved that it had been Troy's grandmother's. The idea that she had enjoyed a happy marriage with this exact ring on for 45 years was a sweet and encouraging thought. Sometimes when I was upset with Troy or a fight was brewing, I would look at her ring and it helped to calm me. The salesclerk's nasal tone broke into my thought process.

"We would be happy to offer you 42.00 for one way transportation to the Philadelphia Airport." After we reviewed all the details, I planted myself in front of a stack of short stories that needed grading. I had to pick up my marking pen three times in the first paragraph. I sighed thinking that was not a good sign.

When Troy got home that evening I was spooning the chicken cutlets out of the sauté pan and setting them on our plates. The rice was hot and ready under its lid, and he produced a bottle of wine to accompany the meal. "I made the reservations for a car to take us to the airport after the reception, today." He carried the plates to the table and we sat across from each other.

"Great." He said in an equivocal tone.

"The wedding is coming up fast don't you think?"

"Yea, are you ready?" He asked cramming a huge bite of chicken in his mouth.

Was I ready? Did he mean were all the plans in place, church, food, cake, decorations, etc.? Or did he mean was I ready to be married to him? Was he really asking himself if he was ready to be married to me? I focused on the plans.

"I think so. Reserving the car was really the last thing on my list. I confirmed all the other details a couple days ago. I'm still waiting for our passports."

"Do you think you mailed them away in plenty of time?" My head involuntarily ticked angrily to the side. Why was it forever on me? For once I would like him to orchestrate and plan a vacation. Shit, I'd settle for him planning the grocery list for a week. I swear I have rendered him useless. He wasn't so dependent when we began dating but he was still living at home then. Sometimes I felt as though I replaced his mom. I can't imagine having someone cook my meals, clean my home, and fold my laundry for an entire day let alone half of a decade.

"According to the US Postal Service website it is taking 2-3 weeks for them to be returned. I sent them 4 weeks ahead of time." I answered dryly.

He just kept eating. The change in my tone hadn't seemed to register on any level with him.

"Vacation is going to be great." His eyes lit up, and he smiled at me. He had that rugged attractiveness to him. Engulfing hands, powerful arms, and a chiseled face. Not many could carry it the way he did. He was not gruff or rough around the edges like other workers. He was a good man.

The rest of dinner was quiet.  Which was fine with me.

## NO!

There was a knock at the door. My ears perked and I
wondered to myself who would be so bold as to knock on our door
at this time of night. I knew it was impossible, but I did envision
Robert standing, hands at his sides, relaxed, calm, and with a
mischievous grin on his face. That would be the most amazing
surprise ever.

Instead I opened the door and was perplexed to see Troy. He
looked out of place. Why was he at my house? His head was
hanging down and his eyes were reddened.

"Hi, Troy. Uhh…can I help you?" I stood at the door not
angling myself to welcome him in. I didn't really know him that
well, my parents weren't at home, and I couldn't think of any reason
why I would want him inside.

He looked up and met my confused and annoyed gaze. His

eyes pierced into mine and then softened; now he looked apologetic. What was going on?

"Robert is dead." His words were simple, short, and he said them crystal clear, but my brain did not register their meaning. My eyes tightened and I froze.

"His mom called me and said I should come tell you."

I put my hand up to stop him. I didn't want to hear anything more he had to say. I just stood frozen. I couldn't think or comprehend anything. And then in a split second my heart broke clean in two. The words he said ripped through my heart, mind, and soul. My throat closed up, my face contorted, my eyes gushed out huge salty tears, and I gripped at the pain in my chest.

We were still standing in the same exact positions when my parents came home seconds, or hours later. I don't have any idea how much time had passed. My mom looked horrified when she saw me. I was standing in the doorway, crying hysterically. There were loud guttural sobs pouring forth, and I was helpless to stop them.

Troy repeated the sickening words to my mom. She went to embrace me but I pushed her away. I didn't want to be touched.

"NOOO!"


I jolted up in bed when I heard the screaming. Troy sat up a moment later and he was shushing me. That was when I realized the screaming was coming from me.

"Are you ok?" He placed his warm hands on my shoulders.

I startled slightly at his touch then forced myself to accept it.

"Huh. Yea. I had a nightmare I guess." I stuttered.

"Do you remember what it was about?" He asked sincere with worry.

"No." I lied.

I laid back down on the pillow and he followed my lead. I rolled over and faced myself to the wall, drawing my legs up to my chest and clutched them tight with my arms. I cried soundlessly, forcing my body to remain still as the pain of years ago shocked through me again. The tears soaked my pillow, and I bit my lip to restrain the sobs threatening to give me away. I allowed myself to remember the memories I had buried so long ago.

Robert had been drinking with his cousin and they got into an accident. No one lived after the car flipped three times and crashed into a utility pole. There was nothing out of the ordinary, just another accident; like any other you read about in the newspaper. Kids being reckless and getting hurt, except for me it had altered every aspect of my existence.

Clutching my knees I relived the memorial service held at his parents house. It was an intimate family gathering that I had never been officially invited to, but I went anyway. I needed to be around others that felt like I had for Robert, that were living the pain that was crippling me. I remember making eye contact with his mom once. She was covered head to toe in black, seated in a chair, shaking as she wept. I wanted to run across the room to her and hug her. I saw us consoling one another. It would have made sense.

She had loved him first, and I would love him last. I needed to cry with someone who loved him as desperately as I did, but she looked up at me as I was contemplating this and gave me a cold stare. She had hated me before, and now perhaps her feelings had strengthened. I was traumatized by the coldness, and I fled from her house. There was a roomful of disapproving stares as I ran but I didn't care. I had hoped to be comforted by sharing this common pain but instead I felt more alone.

I reached out for my car door but tears clouded my vision ,and my hand slipped off just as my fingernails caught the handle's edge. I was wiping my soaked face when I felt a gentle tap on my shoulder. I sheepishly turned around and Troy was standing before me.

"Are you ok?"

I looked at him dumbfounded. Is he freaking kidding me? Do I even look partially alright? I was a complete and utter mess. This was the first time I had been dressed in three days, and the sobering flat hairstyle and black dress my mom had lent me were screaming how miserable I was. My face was drawn and tired with eyes that were permanently swollen from crying. My body was limp and my arms hung at my sides, lifeless. I was precariously holding myself in a vertical position with every bit of energy I could muster though it threatened to crumple to the ground at any moment. Hopefully the wind wouldn't pick up and blow me away.

"I'm fine." I lied.

"You gonna be ok to drive?" He questioned.

"I'll be fine." I flashed a brief false smile and got a good grasp on the door handle before I pulled this time. I wanted to put as much distance between myself and his mom's hateful glare as quickly as possible, so I threw it in gear and took off.

I drove straight home and slumped stupefied in the confines of my room. Robert's presence filled nearly every corner of the space, so I looked down, afraid for any reminders that might catch my attention. I knew the decorations by heart though; pictures of us were littered throughout the room and on the mirrors. Movie ticket stubs, dinner receipts, a coffee cup lid, and other tokens from our relationship were pinned to a bulletin board hanging near my door. The chalkboard wall we had painted together was plastered with juvenile drawings, book quotes we loved, and silly notes to each other. The most noticeable, due to its massive font, was the writing Robert had snuck up on the wall when he came to retrieve my sneakers the morning we drove to the airport. It was an impulsive comment Jane Eyre made to Mr. Rochester after returning home to Thornfield Hall "I am strangely glad to get back again to you; and wherever you are is my home-my only home."

Before, rereading it would evoke a smile at his thoughtfulness now it just caused my breathing to sharpen and elicited a painful stab in my chest. The mementos of us seemed to billow out from themselves until the biting memories were interconnected blanketing the walls with the pain of what would have been. Now it felt as though they were mocking my innocence and trust. I had thought we were invincible before. That we would live out our lives together blissfully happy without a care in the world.

I returned to the present; flannel sheets, legs bunched up to my chest, and Troy snoring inches away. I wondered how difficult the recovery from all that I was allowing myself to remember now would be. It had been so long since I had thought of Robert. Hopefully the pain would be manageable. At least I had not permitted myself to relish the happy memories of him, but I could feel my resolve faltering. I was on a precipice, so enticed to delve into all that was buried but clearly not forgotten. I knew the memories were there waiting for me to allow them to enter my conscious, but I abstained, for tonight at least.

At some point the silent weeping ceased, and I went to sleep. I woke up feeling guilty, like I had cheated on Troy by crying so deeply over Robert with him mere inches from me. Did he knew I had been crying? What would he think? I didn't want to move, afraid he would wake up and confront me about the episode. I lay with my eyes wide open, alert, mildly fearful, and listened intently for his breathing. I wanted to determine whether he was awake or asleep by the pattern of inhaling and exhaling, but I heard nothing. I carefully eased onto my back and saw that his side of the bed was empty with rumpled sheets where he should be laying.

He must have gotten a call from the fire station sometime after I fell asleep. Usually I woke up first when his pager went off, but I must have been out. I got up and took a shower. I felt good, which seemed odd. I expected to be exhausted from the bawling and interrupted sleep; instead, I felt well rested and clear headed.

It was like my body was relieved to finally have been allowed to think about those early days after Robert's death. I had bottled them up for so long and had been adamant about not accessing them for fear of the consequence. Now I saw all that repression had been wearing on me, and my heart was satisfied now that I had acknowledged the affection again. I don't know what good could possibly come of this, but I was thankful that for now I was comforted.

## Wedding

The wedding was in only two weeks which meant I had to plan the curriculum for the time I would be away. I didn't want to be worrying about all the work piling up for me while I was reading on the beach in Mexico. There was an air of contentment that stayed with me as I made progress throughout the day, and I found myself smiling here and there for no reason. I tried convincing myself it was because of my productivity but knew it was more likely related to memories of Robert.

When I looked at the clock and saw it was almost 4:00, my neck muscles tensed slightly. Troy would be home soon. I had forgotten about my earlier fears that he may have sensed my crying and now the guilt crept back in. To allay my conscience, I decided to grill steaks for us. It was his favorite by far, and I didn't mind them. I poured a quick marinade of Italian dressing into a Ziploc bag and mixed it around, coating the steaks thoroughly. While they sat I scrubbed the potatoes and picked out a frozen vegetable. I was just worrying that I was going to have to fire the grill solo when the garage door opening announced his arrival.

"Hey." I greeted him with a big, faintly forged smile. He swung his arm in the door behind him with his lunchbox.

"You made your lunch today?" I was surprised, impressed, and again felt guilty. I always made his lunch.

"Yea. I didn't know if you wanted to get up." He looked at me with a sideways glance, and I was sure he not only knew I had been crying but that it was because of Robert. He seemed to be evaluating me, or maybe I was just being paranoid. How could he possibly know?

"I'm making steak, potatoes, and broccoli for dinner." Ok. That sounded guilty even to me. Now he knows I am trying to make up for something. Shit. Deep breath. I told myself that crying over a friend that died six years ago was not the equivalent of having an affair. But for some reason that is exactly how it felt.

"You grilled the steaks by yourself?" He asked doubtfully.

"No, thankfully your timely arrival saved me from sacrificing my eyebrows again." The joking didn't feel forced. I actually had abstained from the grill in recent months because I had singed my eyebrows and really was scared of a recurrence.

He smiled softly and grabbed the lighter.

"Thanks, Honey." I finished with the sides while he cooked the steaks. I didn't have to peek out the window to know that he would be turning them to produce perfectly aligned grill marks. Outdoor cooking was an art to him, no matter the weather.

We were sharing sincere smiles and little glances throughout dinner, but conversation was sporadic. It was in the vicinity of awkward, and I felt obliged to fill it.

"You got called in early, huh?" I said sympathetically referring to his absence when I awoke this morning.

"Oh. Uh. No, I just couldn't sleep was all, so I figured I could look over that new pump again." He seemed sheepish. Like he had gotten caught, but I knew then that I was the one who had been caught. My paranoia had been justified.

He had known I was crying even with me trying so hard to hide it. I stared at my half eaten dinner and immediately lost my appetite. I was a terrible fiancé for permitting Robert's love to permeate my being again when it was Troy's love and patience that had revived me so long ago. It was as though this past desire was infecting my system, testing me to see if my love for Troy was enough to withstand it. How ridiculous for me to be so changed and affected by a passion that had not existed for years. I swallowed hard, forcing my feelings down again where they belonged.

"That's too bad." I replied airily. I picked up my plate and walked to the sink and was leaning over, rinsing it off when Troy came up and kissed my shoulder.

I could tell he wanted me to turn toward him and motion for him to continue but I couldn't bring myself to. There was too much turmoil within me. It was taking all my will power to not completely surrender to the weakness Robert's memory was causing and verbally analyze the current situation. I just nudged him with my elbow playfully and began loading the dishwasher.

He breathed in rapidly and went into the living room. I closed my eyes and exhaled, not realizing I had been holding my breath ever since his approach. I finished cleaning up the kitchen while Troy put one of his favorite shows on TV. Some sort of action drama that I was not interested in. Sometimes he would guilt me into reading my book on the couch, but I didn't have the mindset to block out screaming and gunshots while I tried to advance my knowledge of teaching success tonight. Instead I filled the tub with hot water. The steam rising off was enticing, and I slowly eased in acclimating my body to the temperature. I let the water envelope me and looked over to the bright red book cover. The eye catching color was not tempting me tonight. I wasn't in the mood for learning about leadership qualities for teachers and closed my eyes instead. I felt alone beneath the water and in the privacy of the bathroom. I let myself relive another memory with Robert.


It was a particularly warm September afternoon and school had just let out. There was an English quiz the following day we were planning to study for in addition to the usual amount of evening homework. Robert was driving my car down the long winding road that led to my development. Fields sat wide on both sides of the road yielding some sort of low lying crop. Our hands were intertwined between the seats, and I wasn't thinking about school, homework, or the quiz. I was happy to be sitting next to him and that was the extent of my thoughts. They were simple, clear, and comforting.

"Stop the car." I said abruptly.

Worry lined his brow as he unraveled our hands. Before he could even look or question me he was heeding my request, slowing the car and pulling it to an abrupt halt on the shoulder.

"Are you ok? What is it?" He threw his gaze to me and relaxed when he saw the mischievous smile covering my face. Before he could say another word I unfastened my seat belt and leapt out of the car, leaving the door ajar in my haste.

I ran into the field, my feet crunching on the ground and my legs slapping the twigs. I put my arms out and let the huge irrigation system spray my hair and clothes. The sun was still radiating full strength, and the beams warmed my moistened body. I felt alive. I ran down the field a ways and when I turned back and saw Robert had gotten sufficiently far in the distance, I sprinted back to him. The fulfillment that overwhelmed me whenever I was returning to him, no matter the length of separation, was awesome. I barely slowed as I approached and crushed my body into him, jamming his back harder into the passenger side door. We mirrored each others stance and were in contact up and down our bodies. I could feel my chest heaving. My face was dewy, and he wiped it with the palms of his hands, pushing the droplets into my hair and letting his hands rest there cradling my face. My smile was full of excitement. He shook his head slightly and then pressed his smirked lips onto mine.

I threw myself into the kiss, enjoying every bit of his mouth as he moved his lips slowly down to my jaw brushing them on my face. His breath trailed onto my neck, and I shivered involuntarily. I could feel his lips draw into a smile at my reaction, and he pulled away to look at me.

"Are you ready to go home now or have you not quenched your urge for sprinkler systems? Do we need to go find another one so that you can fully drench yourself?" He was kidding me, but I knew he would do exactly that if I asked.

I pretended to contemplate his offer, tapping my finger on my chin in faux concentration. "Nah. I am getting a little chilly now."

The breeze went by us as if on cue. He took his hands from my face and pressed one to the small of my back and one higher attempting to completely engulf me with his arms.

"We can't have that. The first step to preventing hypothermia is taking your clothes off. Want me to help?" I rolled my eyes at him.

"Running through the water is one thing, but standing naked on the side of the road is an entirely different situation."

"Just trying to help." He shrugged then peeled us apart, removed his long sleeve shirt, and helped me put it on.


My fingers were starting to shrivel, so I figured I better get out of the tub before Troy felt the need to check that I hadn't drowned. After towel drying I layered on my sweats and began

113

reading on the bed.

I didn't wake up until the next morning, the book creased in my arm. I must have slept solid because it appeared I hadn't moved at all during the night.

I sat up, went to the bathroom, and put my hand to the glass window gauging the temperature outside. It felt icy to the touch, but the trees were still, so I decided an outdoor run was warranted. I wore my thermal layers beneath my yoga pants to protect me from the chill. Gloves and a beanie seemed prudent additions as well. Once I had donned all necessary layers and accessories, I stepped outside. It was chilly for sure, but I knew I would have a good sweat going in no time, so I started up the driveway. My mind cleared, and I concentrated on the coordinated movements of my arms and legs. I was running with music remixed for exercise, and the steady background beat was holding me to a good pace. The chill was burning in my chest, and I was relieved to reach the stop sign and head home.

Troy was wearing a towel around his waist when I walked into the kitchen from the garage.

I took my earplugs out and they hung from the neck of my shirt.

"Will you start my truck, please?" He asked.

"I guess." I grabbed his keys, slightly annoyed, and walked back into the cold. Maybe you wouldn't be running late all the time if you didn't hit snooze every morning.

I made coffee, and while I waited impatiently for it to finish

114

brewing, I made his lunch. He was walking out of the bedroom as I poured my first cup.

"Don't forget tonight is the poker tournament at the station." Definitely a man's idea. Nothing like disguising cards with the guys as a charity event. Everyone pays thirty-five dollars to play cards and drink beer for a few hours all for the benefit of the fire department. Unfortunately, Troy does more of the drinking then the card playing portion.

"Yes. I remember." My mind flashed to last month when I had to pick him up in the middle of the night because he couldn't drive. Well, he of course thought he could, but thankfully, Brian, one of the sober players, had taken Troy's keys earlier in the night.

Brian was a big burly guy with a head of dark hair and biceps like a bouncer. He had to help me get Troy into the car, and that's where he slept because he was passed out by the time I pulled in the garage. I was too tired to drag him out myself, so he woke up cold a few hours later and crawled into bed. I was not looking forward to a repeat of last month and sighed into my coffee mug.

As distasteful as last months scenario was, the promise of a quiet, solitary evening sounded pretty attractive.

After school I worked a little late still trying to get ahead in my work for vacation and decided to treat myself to take out on the way home. I popped in Pretty Women and laid the styrofoam container on my lap. The mushroom ravioli was warm and tender. I was sipping my wine contemplating whether or not to have another glass when I realized it would be safer not to. What if the station

115

called and I needed to pick up Troy again. He is on his own I told myself while I poured another one. If he can't drive then he can sleep there. And with that I enjoyed my next glass and went to bed. I texted him first to say good night though since I hadn't heard from him.

He texted back that he was winning and he would call later. That was a good sign he was being responsible, because he never won cards when he was drinking; he got too arrogant, not a favorable quality in a poker player.

I woke up the next morning and immediately realized Troy had never called me. I checked my phone to be sure, but there were no missed calls or unread texts. A feeling of dread rose from the pit of my stomach, and before I could finish dialing his cell phone number, all the horrible possibilities of what could have happened or where he could be consumed my thoughts.

The phone began to ring as images of Troy took hold; Troy in handcuffs and waiting in a jail cell, or Troy's black truck with its nose stuck in a ditch, or him lying bandaged in a hospital bed. Come on answer.

Nothing.

I dialed the station. One of the advantages of the fire station was someone was always there to answer. I was backing out of the driveway squishing my cell phone to my ear with my shoulder when Brian answered.

"Hey, Brian. It's Sophia. Is Troy there?" I tried to sound calm, but there was an edge to my words. I didn't want Brian to think he was doing Troy any favors by saying he wasn't there if he was passed out on a cot or something.

"No. He left with Billy last night."

"Ok. I'll call him then. Thanks." I went to hang up.

"Actually Billy is here." He said.

"Can I talk to him?" It was embarrassing having to track down your fiancé.

"Sure." I heard a muffled yell for Billy. He must have covered the mouth piece with his hand.

When he got on the phone I dragged just enough information out of him to find out Troy was asleep on the couch at his house. Now that I knew he was safe I got angry. He obviously wasn't as worried about me as I was about him or he wouldn't be so irresponsible. I closed my eyes tight and took a deep breath. It wasn't worth fighting over. It didn't get us anywhere. I consoled myself, thinking that every couple had their own set of problems. No one was as perfect as they appeared to outsiders.

Troy didn't call for the rest of the day. Maybe he was asleep or hung over all day but probably he just didn't feel like talking about last night. At home, I checked my work email and saw a message from the principal.

*Sophia:*

*I know this is unexpected timing, but the board has decided to send one representative to an education summit for the D.C. panel meeting, and I am recommending you.*

*Your meeting is scheduled for first thing Friday morning so that you will be able to return home quickly thereafter. I am sure there are a lot of wedding details you need to complete. Again sorry for any inconvenience, but I see your presence as a necessity.*

*Thank you,*
*Dr. Jossen*

A sinking feeling overtook me, and I shook my head angrily from side to side. Figures. Like there isn't enough on my plate with the wedding plans, honeymoon reservations, and finishing work, now I have to go to D.C. this Friday. I pulled out my calendar and didn't see any appointments that needed to be rescheduled, but I had planned to go out with Jackie for dinner in lieu of a bachelorette party that night.

I heard Troy putting his key in the lock. I must have missed the garage door opening because I was preoccupied with the email. I shut my calendar and figured I could call Jackie tomorrow to cancel.

He walked in, put his key on the hook, gave me a brief *Hey* and peck on the cheek, and kept right on going. The sound of his boots quieted as they moved from the wooden kitchen floor to the carpeted bedroom. His muffled footsteps continued into the bathroom. I heard the water in the shower turn on. The entire time I stared wide eyed at the blank wall.

So its like that. Not only are we not going to fight about his immaturity but he wasn't even going to mention it. I couldn't decide if I was relieved or livid. It would seem that his behavior warranted an apology, but apparently one was not up for the taking. I scoffed at his audacity. He didn't feel culpable for having caused my worry? The disparity between his selfishness and my consideration for his feelings was ridiculous. I had been sick with worry that I had caused him hurt when I was crying the other night, but he leaves, doesn't call, and is dead for all I know, and he doesn't feel a pang of regret or remorse. How can it possibly be that he is so self involved that the consequences of his actions on anyone other than himself are not considered? I swallowed hard, put dinner on my plate, and ate alone in the living room.

I woke up the next morning with Troy's arm draped over me and I hugged it tighter to my chest. I was over our lack of a fight. We never really fought and I didn't want that to change days before our wedding. That would seem a bad omen. I continued to hold his arm braced between mine as I remembered a fight Robert and I had had.


The bell rang signaling the end of math...thank God. Math was by far my least favorite subject, and I was sure the least likely to have any significance in the future what with the well known inventions of calculators and computers. I slung my bag over my shoulder briskly, having already packed my book while Mr. Pollock was finishing the last equation. Did he really believe this junk was important, or was it all a ruse to try and convince the students. Robert was still packing his bag, having waited until the last moment, making sure he absorbed every detail the teacher was relaying. I sat on his desk, and he poked the band patch I had sewn on last night.

"New addition?" He said with his eyebrows arched.

"Yup. If you listened to them I am sure you would like them."

"I am sure you do think that." He teased.

I stuck my tongue out.

"Ooh, feisty."

"You say that like it's something new."

He put his bag over his shoulder and reached for my hand.

"Well, while you're in such a delightful mood I need to tell you something."

"Dun, Dun, Dah" I tried to make the ominous interlude sound from Law and Order to emphasize his preface.

"Chandra wants me to go the masquerade ball with her."

I ripped our hands apart. I didn't move. My feet were planted shoulder width apart, with my knees stiff. Chandra was a bubbly gossipy girly girl two years older than us. I was stunned. How could he like her? She was so…so…typical. Ugh. How could he?

He put his hands up, palms out like he was surrendering.

"Whoa whoa whoa. It's not like that."

"It's not like what? Did I misunderstand? Are you not going

to take her to the dance?" I was suppressing a scream and was barely losing the battle with myself.

"She knows we are going as friends and I am doing it as a favor really."

"Oh, well in that case. No problem. You want me to come over and cook your dinner. I could chauffeur you both. I know, how about I be your photographer for the evening. What service can *I* provide to make this evening more memorable for the *two of you!*" I had progressed down the emotional spectrum from anger to tears, and they were threatening to spill from my eyes right there as we stepped into the hallway.

Robert took my hand and ushered me from public view in the hall to the outdoor picnic tables used by students on warm days.

"Soph, are you really that pissed?" He questioned.

"Pissed? No this embarrassing display has all been for your entertainment. Hope you enjoyed it!" I screamed this time, now that we were not confined within the schools walls. He was usually so in tune with my feelings that this complete lack of insight was astounding. "How could you?"

"I told you it is just as friends." He walked towards me with his arms out ready to comfort me.

"No!" I shoved him away with my fists. How could he not be getting this? I didn't have the restraint to calm down and explain exactly how audacious it was of him to not only accompany another girl to a dance while he is going out with me but for it to be an older girl, a pretty girl, and a black girl. And to not even consult me. I pushed with all my weight against him and stormed off toward my car.

Robert had pulled me so quickly through the halls that everyone else was just now exiting the school and heading to the parking lot. I didn't run, afraid to draw even more attention to myself if that was possible. I reached my car and dropped into my seat slamming the door behind me. The band he and I had been referring to earlier was streaming in my car, and I cranked it up as I sped free of the school zone. I let the cacophony pouring from the speakers drown out my thoughts.

I ran into the house and took the stairs two at a time up to my room. I threw myself onto the bed and covered my head with a pillow. I was seeing visions of Robert and Chandra at the dance. His flawless appearance next to her good looks. They would make an attractive couple. Their matching skin as they skimmed each others arms while dancing. It made me sick. Whether she was into him now or not she would be flaunting him around to her friends at the dance. I can just hear her teasing comments as she mingles with the other seniors escorted by *my* boyfriend. "I hope Sophia isn't too upset. Or we better not dance too close I don't want your girlfriend getting jealous."

Aaah. I was just about to let the scream in my head escape from my lips when my cell phone rang. My heart skipped hoping it was Robert but I saw it was Jen.

"Hey." I said reluctantly.

"Hey. You alright? I heard you got into a fight with

Robert?" She wasn't prying.

"Yea. I'm ok. It's alright, really." I wasn't trying to hide anything from her. She, as always, was sincere with her concern. I never had to worry that she was trying to collect gossip. I just didn't want to explain the situation. Mostly because I was embarrassed that the boyfriend I gushed over had made such an insensitive blunder.

"I heard what happened in the hallway. I can't imagine what he was thinking."

Great. The news of my dramatic reaction had spread and now everyone was probably scrutinizing each word of our fight. Just the sort of attention I wanted (heavy sarcasm).

"I know. You don't think I am over reacting do you? He said they are just going as friends but still." I pressed.

"Totally. No he's wrong, flat out."

We bashed his stupidity for a while until I was sufficiently satisfied that he was an ass and that Jen agreed. I closed the phone and looked at my book bag. There was no way I could possibly concentrate on anything in there, so I crammed my earplugs in and let my "girly-goth" music, as Robert described it, soothe me. I didn't have it loud enough to completely curtail all trains of thought though, and I found myself annoyed that even though I was angry at Robert, I still wanted him here. That was adding to my frustrations. I was glad Jen had called, and it felt good to vent to her but ultimately it was him that I wanted.

Why hadn't he chased after me? I am not that fast, he could

have easily been to my car before I pulled out. I would have pounded and screamed and then melted into him and forgiven him. I just needed the chance to hurt first. How is it that even when you are so wounded by someone they are still the one you want around? I was pathetic to need him so entirely. I wanted him here so I could yell at him until my throat was dry and my voice cracked. I wanted him to wipe my tears and to explain what the hell he was thinking taking Chandra to the dance. Everything was running through my mind at lightning speed as I analyzed the miniscule bumps on the minusculeceiling in my room.

"Can I come in?" My eyes darted to the door.

It was Robert.

"Do you want help picking out your outfit for the dance?" I fired back.

"Please let me explain. Can I come in and talk to you?" He was pleading.

"I can hear you fine from there." I would not give in so easily even though I was smiling to myself because he had come to talk me. He was right where I wanted him. Here so I could push him away. That sounds crazy, but I can't help the insanity my addiction for him causes.

"Fine. If this is the way you want to do it."

"I don't want to do this at all. Do not put this on me. This is all your fault." I spat back.

"Ok. Ok. Look, Chandra is dating Ricky and he was supposed to come up that weekend for the dance but at the last minute had to pull out. He guilted me into it on the phone last night, and after punching him and all I felt bad enough to agree. See it is completely platonic. I in no way meant to upset you."

"Well you did."

"Yes. I picked up on that fact way back in the hallway outside class when you were throwing daggers at me with your eyes...I really am sorry." He finished off his sarcastic comment with quiet sincerity, and I knew he was sorry, but I wasn't done yet. The heat of the fight was calming, but I wanted him on his knees.

"You should have talked to me first. You should have asked my opinion, which by the way would have been NO. Why did you tell me so nonchalantly in the hallway? And why didn't you run after me to explain instead of letting me seethe for the last two hours?"

"I obviously should have spoken with you first and am considering checking each detail of my life with you after this experience. Seriously, I will call before dressing in the morning."

"Actually I think you do that better without my opinion." I offered. We were both smiling through the closed door at each other.

"I thought you might attack me with your car if I tried to stop you after school, so instead I found Chandra and told her the plan was off. There is no favor worth upsetting you like this. She was really upset. I mean she cried and called Ricky on the spot."

Now I was really smiling. I loved that he had remedied the problem without me having to nag him.

"Can I come in now, pleeaase?" He pleaded.

That sounded like the verbal equivalent of groveling, so I surrendered and crossed the floor to the door and opened it. He was leaning forward with his hands braced on either side of the door jam and his head was hung down. Damn he was hot. His head shot up in surprise when I opened the door, and his eyes met mine. Then he reached for me. He brought my body to his pulling my feet up off the ground and hugged me fully. Simultaneously he walked us further into my room and swung the door shut behind us. Our bodies meshed together, and I was hugely aware of vital points of contact. Our legs aligned and our midriffs crushed together as he held me tight at the small of my back. We kissed deep and strong while he fumbled us backwards onto my bed. He landed on top of me. His smell was amazing, and I breathed in his scent as his lips grazed the length of my neck and rested below my ear. He pulled his torso up with his arms locked straight and looked at me.

"Maybe I should get you jealous more often." And then he turned over onto his right side, kissed my shoulder, and ran his hand across my stomach. His touch thrilled me and filled my head. He grasped my hip, firm, and pulled me on top of him. I let my weight fall onto him and smoothed my hand along his head and then brought our lips together again. He skimmed up my thighs and again grasped my hips as he pushed deeper into my kiss. I could have kissed and touched him like this for an eternity, but my mom interrupted with a dinner announcement.

"Soph, dinner time. Robert, are you staying?" He tugged

his lips from mine.

"Yes. Thank you." He called back. "As long as that's ok with you?" He questioned teasingly.

I glared at him and pecked him on the lips one more time before peeling myself away. I went to stand up to straighten my hair and clothes before sitting at the dinner table, but he held tight to my hand. He was sitting on the bed looking up at me where I stood.

"Hold on. First I have something to ask you. Annasophia, will you go to the dance with me?"

I looked at him puzzled. "What do you mean?"

"Well, technically you would be going with Dell, but I would definitely be your date. This way we can go to the dance and Chandra gets to go to. What do you say?"


Robert and I were walking through the halls the next day when I felt Tina, Chandra's best friend, glare at me from her locker. I suppressed the urge to stick my tongue out, though I found the idea incredibly tempting. Instead I just grasped his right hand with mine and pulled his arm around my shoulder. He knew what I was doing and played along.

He bent his lips to my ear in a seductive manner "You have nothing to prove to her; I am yours totally and completely."

I had never felt possessive of Robert until I felt my position was vulnerable. It had tortured me to picture him with Chandra, especially the irksome comments I imagined her making in regard to taking my boyfriend out. Whether they were going as friends or not, and regardless that he was doing his cousin a favor, I had felt threatened for that brief period of time.

The episode actually ended with the opposite effect. His quick solution of going back on his commitment with her further solidified our relationship, and she ended up being the jealous party. I didn't have a problem with Chandra until she was audacious enough to assume having Robert escort her to the dance wouldn't be any of my concern. She had already run her mouth to a few of her friends that Robert wasn't really into me, and she had to eat her words. I did get a certain level of satisfaction from the way the scenario ended up.

I smiled and felt a little childish flaunting us in that way, but what he said was true, so why not display it. Really it was for Chandra's benefit. I didn't want her clinging to any ridiculous hope that he might change his mind.

I was enjoying Robert's arm around me when the present restored, and I remembered it was Troy's arm that was holding me. Suddenly the embrace felt confining instead of comforting. Why had Robert's mess up hurt me so much more than Troy's redundant ones? Troy's transgressions never seemed to evoke the powerful emotions that Robert's did. I told myself it was because I was older and more mature than the teenager I had been back then. I had learned from my previous fated relationship. I tucked the thought away not wanting to delve too deep. I had a sneaking suspicion I wasn't ready to face the answer. I stretched and released myself from Troy's hold.

# Bipolar

I didn't need to run because I had done that the previous morning. I could read a few chapters in bed because it was still early but decided to get up instead. The coffee brewed while I put Troy's lunch together. I opened his lunch box and had to remove the warm ice pack and trash from yesterday's before I could fill it. I clenched my teeth. You'd think he could at least empty it out at the end of the day.

I poured my coffee and positioned myself at the barstool as his alarm beeped for the first time, beginning his snooze routine. I looked outside at the frost coating the blades of grass. I hoped there wasn't going to be some freak snowstorm that would completely f-up all the wedding plans.

I pulled out my calendar and surveyed the week ahead while

pouring my second cup of coffee. I rolled my eyes when I saw the square for Friday was covered with my scribble: WASHINGTON. I hadn't had a chance to tell Troy about the meeting, but I didn't foresee him being bothered by it. His boots clunked onto the kitchen floor announcing his entrance.

"Morning." He said simply. No trace of regret lined his face. I was still expecting a hint of an apology even if he hid it in his words or actions. You know a kiss, comment, or hug intending to show he was sorry.

I got nothing.

"Morning." I turned toward him "Dr. Jossen emailed me yesterday and I have to be in D.C. for a meeting on Friday. It's scheduled for the morning so I should be back later in the day though I can't be sure of the time." My tone was flat.

"Ok. Everything gonna be ok with the wedding plans?" I don't know why but his sudden concern for the wedding rubbed me wrong. He had been more than willing for me to show him invitations, flowers, etc to help me choose but hadn't had any responsibilities besides offering his opinion. Now a week before the wedding he is questioning my judgment because I am leaving for a mandatory work meeting?

"It's pretty much on autopilot now. I confirmed everything last week, so there's nothing to do but wait."

"Sounds good." He grabbed his lunchbox with one hand.

I was planted in front of the coffee pot like an alcoholic seated at a bar. He leaned across me and brushed my shirt while he

130

reached for the to go cup I had poured him. He straightened his position and kissed my cheek. I was still annoyed with him and his kiss did nothing for me. I slurped another bit of coffee as he turned and walked out the door.

The day was speeding past, and I was surprised when I packed my bag that I had forgotten to call Jackie during my lunch break. I had better do it now. She can ramble though, and I didn't want to have to cut her short. I saw she was signed in for instant messaging online and decided to send her a note instead.

I wrote:

*I gotta go to D.C. Friday for work and don't think I'll be able to squeeze in the bachelorette dinner you had planned.*
*Sorry Soph*

She responded:

*Can I come? We can do a girl night and more of a traditional bachelorette soiree. Jackie.*

That idea had not crossed my mind but sounded worthwhile.

*Let's do it.* I wrote back

*Great. How about I see if Jen can make it up from Baltimore.*

*Ooh. Yes, please.*

This work commitment was sounding a whole lot better now with Jackie and possibly Jen joining in.


My evening with Troy went by uneventfully, and the next morning I was standing in my closet pulling my sweaty running

131

outfit off when I surveyed my clothes thinking about what I could wear Friday night with Jen and Jackie. I was really looking forward to an evening out and hoping Jen would be able to make it. She had two kids, ages one and three, so she didn't get out much. It would be awesome for us to have a last hurrah together before the wedding.

I stood under the water wondering what sort of plans we would have for the evening. Dinner for sure. I hoped we would go dancing. I didn't have great moves or rhythm, but I had always thought my enthusiasm made up for those shortcomings. Excitement was brewing inside of me. I was feeling giddy and realized it had been a while since I had something on the horizon that inspired such a reaction.

There was nothing in my closet jumping out at me, so I thought maybe I would go shopping and try to find something fun. I was tucking my fitted white sweater into my flare legged dress khaki pants when I caught a glimpse of my outfit in the mirror. I looked like a Lands End add and not in a good way. Suddenly the shirt felt restricting and uncomfortable. I was picking which shoes to wear when I saw my brown converse sneakers. I hadn't worn them in an eternity but felt the need to now. I posed in the mirror and a smirk snuck onto my face. I walked out of my room with an added bounce in my step.

I felt different all day. I considered it ridiculous that putting on sneakers had caused me to feel so daring. I guess that showed how straight laced I had become.

I was sautéing shrimp in a cream sauce when Troy came in

that night. He noticed my converse right away.

"Haven't seen those in a while?" He looked confused.

"I know." I shrugged my shoulders nonchalantly and poured the contents of the pan atop spaghetti noodles.

His eyes seemed to be scrutinizing me, looking for a change other than my shoes I suppose. I guess he came up empty because he didn't comment on my appearance any more.

"How was work?"

"Fine. You?" I questioned.

"Nothing to speak of really." He replied. "This looks really good." He grabbed both of our plates and carried them to the table.

"I told Jackie I couldn't go to dinner with her Friday night because of work and she proposed coming with me, so we wouldn't have to cancel." I said cheerily.

"I didn't remember that you were going out Friday night."

"Troy, I told you weeks ago she wanted to treat me to dinner the Friday before the wedding. Anyway it sounds like this is going to work out better, and she is trying to get Jen to join us also. Wouldn't that be great?" I raised my eyebrows at him.

"Yea. You guys would have fun." He gestured with his fork before putting a bite into in his mouth.

"I think so. We haven't all gotten to hang out so long. It will be fun for us all to be together, you know?" I smiled.

"Well, Jen is going to make it to the wedding too, right?" He looked at me.

"Oh. Yea of course. Uh...I mean just the three of us you

know. The wedding is going to be so hectic and with family and friends so I won't get to spend a lot of quality time with them."

"Right." He acquiesced.

I stood up to clear the table when Troy took the plate from my hands.

"I got it. Why don't you take a bath or something? You cooked, I'll clean."

"Thanks, babe."

I sank into the steam, and after a couple minutes of warm pleasure, I picked up my book. This was not the type I planned to read on the beaches in Mexico, so I needed to just hunker down and finish it already. Usually I enjoyed books involving teaching or education, but I could not get into this one. I am not sure if it was the author or content, but I had to give myself a pat on the back each time I finished a chapter to encourage myself to continue.

I was still toasty from the bath when I sat on the couch next to Troy in my sweats. We were definitely past pretenses, and I didn't think twice about how I dressed around the house. I guessed we were like an already long married couple in that way. I knew grown women who wouldn't brush their teeth in view of their husbands which seemed bizarre. Modesty had never been an issue between us. Troy had seen me in horrible shape in our early days, and so I never felt concern over how I looked to him.

Surely I looked far better than just after Robert died. I had cried spontaneously for weeks. It unnerved anyone who was with me; not knowing when I might fall into a full blown cry fest. It would be a surprise even to me. The episodes were embarrassing, but I was powerless to stop them. Sometimes it felt good to cry over him, like I was releasing a portion of the pain that was pervasive within me. At night I would practically suffocate myself trying to muffle the screams that slipped from inside me. I learned how to control some of the bawling and only stifled moans would escape; eventually I was able to choke back even those.

It was draining for people to be around me. I was an abyss, sucking in any positive energy. It was a foreign feeling to me, far from the boisterous and joyful person I had been only weeks prior. I wanted to hang out with my friends so that I could listen to them kid and talk, but I didn't want to participate. I craved contact that would prove to me that life was continuing even with my heart vehemently denying it. It was all I could do to just sit and breathe. I was physically present but not engaged with any activities going on. I was a spectator in my own life.

Troy was the only one that regularly made the effort to visit me. It was comforting to be around someone that had loved Robert even if it wasn't of the same caliber. He and I swapped memories, and it was healing. Perhaps Troy considered spending time with me his penance for allowing his and Robert's friendship to become distant. It was a long process, but Troy was committed to seeing me through my recovery.

Troy adjusted his position on the couch, pulling me from analyzing our history any further and patted the cushion in front of him. I laid down beside him, and he rested his arm on my chest and chin on my head. Our breathing matched, and I was content.

I had my bag packed as early as the students the next afternoon, wanting to get outside as soon as possible. It was warm even with the wind blowing, and I had my window open in the car driving home. The radio was on but I wasn't really paying attention to it. I was thinking how fast the wedding had crept up on us. It was Wednesday, which meant in a week and a half Troy and I would be married. This deduction made me apprehensive, but I am not sure why. Like I had told Troy, everything was on autopilot from here. Practically all that was left to do was show up.

I was digging for my cell phone in my purse to call Jackie when the radio song caught my attention. I suddenly had the urge to blare it. I turned the dial up, put all the windows down, and sang with gusto. My tapping on the wheel progressed to full on banging, and my dancing became more animated while I remained completely oblivious to my surroundings until I slowed for a red light. I looked over and saw a couple teenagers in the car adjacent to mine looking my way; they had been entertained by my show. I was not deterred even slightly and continued to enjoy myself performing what felt like suave moves but probably appeared as spastic gyrations until the song ended.

I was still smiling to myself when I pulled into the department store parking lot. I felt like energy had sparked within me, and I was unashamedly gleeful. I let my mood pervade the space around me, and flung the door open singing carelessly.

I hadn't bought anything besides work clothes in a while and was looking forward to shopping. I was in the mood for something different and fun. I searched rack after rack sliding the hangers recklessly while singing the chorus over and over. My hype was starting to drain a little as I realized there was nothing here that would compliment my attitude. I should have been tipped off immediately when I set eyes on the mannequin layered with gaudy gold jewelry and a boxy white number.

I stepped out and let the sun's rays beat on my arms, absorbing each speck of heat. It seemed to mimic the flame that had sparked in me. I reached into my bag to unclip my keys from their designated spot when my phone blared. I reached in my back pocket and saw it was Jackie.

"Hey!" I exclaimed.

"Hey!" She imitated my enthusiasm.

"Shut up!" I said without a hint of annoyance.

To the tune of the toddler taunt "nanny nanny boo boo" she sang. "I just talked to Jen and she is coming."

"What…Awesome." I squealed.

"I know. What are you doing? Are you out of work already?"

"Yup. I wanted to go shopping for Friday night but haven't had any luck."

"Oooh. I should probably get something new too." I could tell she was mentally designing an outfit.

"Oh, please. I should probably just shop in your closet and

137

save myself the money." Saying Jackie had a well stocked closet was being modest.

"You are more than welcome. If you do have any luck let me know so I can check it out." She instructed.

"Will do. Talk to you later." I tucked my phone back into my pocket.

Walking across the parking lot I unhooked my keys from the d-ring and before opening my door glanced around. That's when I saw the blue and white thrift store sign. I used to have a lot of luck with thrift stores and had just gotten out of the habit in recent years. It was clear across the parking lot but I decided to walk anyway.

I swung open the glass door and the stale air hit me. It wasn't unpleasant, it just didn't contain that sterile scent that department stores possess.

Racks were clearly marked with signs hanging above. I didn't really need pants and was generally luckier with shirts anyway so I started digging through the short sleeve rack beneath the sign announcing Women's shirts $3.25 in stark white lettering. There were two full racks the length of a pickup truck, with shirts grouped by color rather than size. After an hour and a half of searching, choosing, trying on, and repeating the process, I paid 33 dollars for a brown grocery bag full of new to me clothes. Replacing my debit card and setting my wallet in its designated spot I looked out the picture frame glass windows that lined the entire facing of the store. Rain was splattering down. Well, shit.

I expected to be agitated but I wasn't. A fact that did not

escape my notice. My buoyant mood would not be so easily dulled, and I dashed out into the shower. My speed wouldn't save me from being drenched, but I ran anyway because it felt good. Until the paper bag could not withstand the beating rain any longer and one seam burst open. A couple items hit the pavement. Still not deterred I kicked them and impressed myself when I caught them mid air.

The bag was in shambles, along with its contents and new owner, as I slung all parties into my car. I looked in the mirror and a huge smile plastered my face. My first thought of *what was going on with me* was immediately followed up with *who cares*. I decided to enjoy my recent lapse with sanity and turned the radio dial searching for a station. I skipped the first two favorites knowing they were news stations. The next was having a commercial break and the fourth was too slow. The fifth and last button was dead air. Really, I had never even programmed it. That was just sad. I hit seek and pulled out my old CD pouch.

The familiar yellow color on a disc caught my eye, and I decided to throw it back old school. I shook and bumped in my wet seat the whole way home. Troy's truck was in the driveway. I parked in the garage and started piling the moist clothes into my arms. I could hardly manage all of them and had one tucked under my chin.

I banged my toe on the door to call Troy's attention and waited for him to open it.

Nothing.

I banged my toe again.

Nothing.

An expletive fired through my head and I dropped the armful at my feet. I'll just do it myself. I shook my head around like I was talking pointedly to someone, but it was all in my brain. I pushed the door in and started the washer located right at the entrance. I was throwing the wet and now dirty items from the garage floor into the basin.

"Hey, Sophia." I didn't look up. I grabbed for the detergent swirled a cup full on top the clothes.

"You have anything you need washed?" I asked dryly turning the dial for the regular wash cycle.

"No, I don't think so. You alright?" He pointed to my wet hair and the clothes clinging to my body. I realized that having to drop my clothes onto the dirty garage floor had finally been enough to extinguish my good mood. Discovering I was in a bad mood just pissed me off further. Ugh.

"What happened?" He pressed.

"The bag broke so I had all the clothes in my arms, but you didn't answer the door when I kicked it. I had to drop them in the garage and open the door myself." I started stripping off my wet layers, in an angry, not a sexy way, and adding them to the load as I ranted.

Once I had down-spiraled into this cranky mood I just couldn't get rid of it. I practically growled when I spoke to Troy and sat like a worthless lump all through dinner. For the second time today I asked myself *what was going on with me,* but the circumstances generating the thought process were complete opposites. Earlier being drenched by rain couldn't ruin my elation, and now only hours later, I was sulking on the couch. It was infuriating. Maybe I was bipolar, seemed prevalent enough. Or maybe it was just hormones. Damn I hated them. I finally decided that perhaps I was just tired. I had been dealing with a lot between work and the wedding. I climbed into bed early and fell asleep.

## Washington

I was folding laundry on Thursday after school when my phone rang.

"What are you doing, right now?" Jackie sounded frantic and excited. Her boisterousness made me anxious.

"Nothing. What is it?"

That's when I heard a car pull up outside and repetitive short honks.

"What are you doing?" I asked incredulous.

I walked over to the window and pulled the curtain back when I heard the house door from the garage open and close.

"Come on. We're going...now!" she shouted. I still had the phone to my ear when I wheeled around and faced her in the kitchen.

"What?" I was lost.

"Come on. I know Miss planned and precise already has her bag packed for tomorrow morning. Why wait? I'm stealing you early. We're going to D.C. now, and we'll get our hair and nails done so we're our most amazing selves tomorrow night."

I loved her spontaneity, and her excitement was infectious. I rolled my eyes at her comment about my being packed, but pointed to the blue case sitting by the door. She grabbed my arm with one hand and my bag with the other and yanked us both out the door. I called Troy and explained my being kidnapped. He seemed genuinely happy and told me to have a great time.

I had grabbed my CD pouch out of my car before Jackie peeled out of town and we rocked out to the songs of our high school days with fervor.

"I feel like we're sixteen again." I was full on seat dancing with my arms swaying above my head.

"You have the outfit to match." She said pointing at me.

I was wearing one of my thrift store finds. A green little league boys shirt over top, a white hooded tee with jeans, and my converse. I had worn my sneakers practically every day since I had dusted them off in my closet.

"Hey. This is thrift store chic." I laughed. "I think I finally overdosed on my cardigans."

"You and me both, honey."

If it wasn't so cool outside I probably would have been sweating when we pulled into the hotel's valet lane.

I couldn't help but notice my well manicured nails while making notes as another teacher discussed the positive impact involving parents more in the teaching process has had on grades in her school. Jackie was surprised when I chose the black polish, but I really liked it. The woman with cat eyeglasses was droning on about daily email notification from teachers to parents her school had instituted. That sounds great, I thought to myself. Just what I want to do with my Friday away from the school. Call twenty parents that are more concerned with what social events they are attending that weekend than with what some lowly teacher has to tell them about little Emma not sharing her play dough. Could this meeting be over already?

I looked towards the exit, willing myself beyond the doors. I squinted my eyes, focusing through the tiny windows in each door and out into the lobby when I saw two figures jumping around and flailing their arms. It was a moment later that I smiled to myself when I recognized the figures as Jen and Jackie. I wondered how long they had been trying to catch my attention. I stood up quietly and excused myself. I was so excited to see Jen and gave her a big hug as soon as I walked through the door. Jackie explained they were going shopping and to call when my meetings were done. I did my best to make them feel awful for leaving me at the dreadful meeting but had no luck.

A solid two hours later I practically leapt from the table when we were dismissed. I was hitting send on my cell phone before I had even exited the doors. I walked outside, and goose bumps popped up on my arms as a chilly wind swept my hair. While the phone rang in my ear, I saw them both coming up the sidewalk each carrying multiple bags, presumably of clothes.

"Didn't have any luck, huh?" I teased.

"She is a maniac. Seriously dangerous." Jen said pointing accusingly at Jackie. "We're going to have to eat McDonalds for dinner tonight because she made me blow my whole budget before noon."

"You'll be thanking me every time you put one of those outfits on. The dress is especially cute and totally worth subjecting your children to eating Ramen Noodle dinners for the next month."

They continued up the steps, and I helped carry their bags. They promptly unloaded everything on the beds to review all the finds. They had both bought dresses for tonight and now I wanted one. We headed out of the hotel, and this time the whole trio was present for the shopping trip. Jen refused to go to any new stores, afraid she would spend more money, so we copied their morning route. At the third store I saw the dress I wanted before we had even walked inside. In the display window a mannequin was glowing in a yellow strapless dress that stopped mid thigh and had a single layer of black crinoline poking out the bottom. It was perfect.

I felt amazing as we passed thru the lobby that evening freshly primped, showered, and shaved in our new dresses. Jen hadn't changed much since high school even after factoring in a husband, house, and two kids. I wondered why the last six years had changed me so much. I didn't let myself answer. Tonight was for fun not scrutiny.

We were in step with one another as we talked and laughed past the front desk, out the doors, and into the dusk. A taxi delivered us to an asian fusion restaurant. Our seats were at the sushi bar, where Jen quickly caught the attention of two rollers preparing the fish which looked more like art than dinner. Like I said, nothing much had changed since high school. We shared a huge plate of sushi, polished off two large sakes, and when I feared my breathing pattern may be impacted by the volume I had consumed, a dessert plate was passed to Jen by one sushi chef. He was thin, Asian, and attractive.

I was waddling out of the door when I said "I am not sure how much dancing I can do with an ocean full of fish swelling up my stomach."

"Oh, don't you dare back out. I never get to go dancing and you two are taking me out." Jen returned.

"I thought this was my party?" I said smartly.

"Not if you're going to try and punk out on me. So where are you taking me dancing?" She concluded.

I turned to Jackie for advice, and she gave us a mischievous smile.


"Room service." A polite voice came through the hotel room door.

I was lying on my stomach with my face smashed into a pillow. I lifted my head and looked around disoriented. Memories of the previous evening came streaming back to mind. There had been dancing, sweating, and a lot of men. Jackie had taken us to a gay bar explaining the music would be better than the crap the other bars usually played. She had been right. The music was great and we weren't interrupted by any guys trying to pick us up. We weren't their type.

"We didn't order anything." I shouted back in a not so polite voice.

"It was ordered for you." Again professionally polite.

Apparently this was going to have to be dealt with while in an upright position. I pushed off the bed, felt my sore muscles, and noted the small spot on the white pillowcase where I had been drooling. Must have been a good dream.

I opened the door to find a waiter holding a covered tray with what I gathered was food, and more importantly coffee, unless my olfactory nerves were playing tricks on me.

"Sir. We didn't order anything." *But leave the coffee and nobody gets hurt* was how the sentence continued in my head.

"Yes. An order was called in for you last night by Troy Jackson."

With that I stepped aside. I had frozen, surprised by Troy's thoughtfulness and was still standing with my hand on the door when the waiter smiled at me and walked out after placing the tray on the table.

I surveyed the items before taking a mug of coffee over to the window and sat with my legs curled up on the seat with me.

Neither Jen nor Jackie were stirring, and I didn't want to cut short their slumbers by letting more sun in, so I stared out through the crack between the curtain panels. I felt safe here. The hotel room seemed a refuge with my friends ready to shield or shelter me. It's great we can still have so much fun together, but above all I treasured knowing they would stand by me no matter the circumstances. Their loyalty was unwavering. It was with their presence providing complete security I let my mind wander to territories I had refused to venture into over the last couple weeks. My subconscious had been trying relentlessly to make me confront the memories but I wouldn't. I wasn't sure what I would uncover and until now hadn't felt secure enough to probe. I sipped my coffee and let myself get lost in thought.

Troy and I would be married in one week from today, and that fact sat heavy on me. I thought back to the beginning of our story. He had been a constant presence in my life ever since Robert's death. Troy had been my rock as I waded through months of grief and tears. He had coddled and comforted me, and I clung to his support and friendship. Slowly we fell into a routine. He called in the evenings to check on me, walked me to classes, and took Robert's place next to me at the lunch table. Somehow, over a period of months, it seems we began dating. I honestly don't know how it happened, it just did. I don't think I was ever consulted in the decision. I was just a pawn in my own life, a hollow shell of who I had been. It seemed logical that we would be a couple. The friend and the girlfriend leaning on each other as they grieved their mutual loss.

As I further analyzed our relationship it struck me that what we had was more of a glorified friendship that grew out of our shared love of Robert and the pain over his death. It was Robert that had initially brought us together and formed our bond. With Troy's patience and insistence, my brain forced my heart and soul to heal. We were compatible in many ways, but I see now that I never let him enter my being the way Robert had been a part of me. Troy's love was merely permitted to orbit the space that Robert's had once ruled. This realization scared me. I had managed to fool myself so thoroughly into believing he and I were in love. We weren't. We loved each other, but the indescribable link Robert and I shared was absent.

In many ways Troy was ideal. We wouldn't have been able to fall into a routine and slide effortlessly into a relationship had we not truly been good friends. He proved his commitment and compassion as he took care of me through my heartache. He showed selflessness tending to my needs as I gradually healed. The thought dawned on me, were those months of consideration and concern for my well being enough to last a lifetime full of marriage? And *if* our friendship was of a sturdy enough quality to build a life, *should* we?

A tear welled in my eye, and as I reached to wipe it, Jen caught my hand and instantly saw what I had been trying to hide from myself. Confusion sat plain on my face, and she recognized everything I had been masking. Her face softened; she sat next to me and released my hand to adjust her position.

"What is it?" She asked gently but firm. She wanted the truth.

"I don't know what to do." I confessed. Saying the words that had been swirling deep within me over the last couple weeks was liberating and scary.

"Robert has been on my mind constantly. I dream about him every night and my thoughts wander to him every day. I woke up screaming last week with Troy next to me, and cried silently, reliving the memory of his death. I don't know what is going on."

"I think that seems natural." She offered.

"Really?" I was shocked at her quick acceptance.

"Robert was your first love. It seems reasonable to me that his memories would resurface now, when you are about to be married."

I pondered this while Jen perused the breakfast tray. I suppose it could be a form of cold feet, which is common to most couples. Except for me it was an uncanny recollection of my first love and our tragic ending that was causing doubts. I hadn't expected her to explain away all this turmoil so simply. I could see what she was saying, but did she comprehend the depth to which I was being affected? I think if she knew the magnitude that these memories had taken up in my conscious she would understand better the chaos inside me. My being was consumed with Robert again as it was so many years ago.

"Do you love Troy?" She asked flat out settling into the seat beside me.

"Yes." I paused. It was hard to say the words. "But not like I love Robert."

There it was. I had said it, come clean. It had not escaped my notice that I had used the present tense, saying love. I did still love him. I was a horrible person for feeling this way. It wasn't fair to Troy. It kind of ticked me off at Robert. I had trudged through tears and pain to become who I was, and now it was crumbling all around me. His presence was haunting me, and its grasp was unnerving.

"You don't have to feel guilty for loving Robert. Troy knows that you do. He doesn't expect you to rid him of your memory. He will always be a part of you and that is not something to feel guilty for. Carry him with you wherever you go, just don't let him stop you from going in the first place." She reasoned.

Again her reaction confounded me. She was permitting me to love Robert but marry Troy. The idea that Troy knew and approved of my continued love of Robert was a bizarre thought. How could he be so generous? Why would he be? Would it be fair to Troy? Marry him while still loving Robert?

That bared the second question. Could my memories of our love sustain me for the rest of my life with Troy? Was it enough for me? There was no magical pull, heated attraction, or palpable connection between Troy and me. Will I ever have that again with someone?

"What did I miss?" Jackie came up behind me and pulled me from my train of thought.

"Nothing. Troy sent us breakfast." Jen replied as she gave me a knowing look that clearly said *see, he is a good guy*.

But I already knew that.

"Sweet." Jackie turned backwards and grabbed a croissant and coffee off the tray.

Jen headed toward the shower seemingly done with our mini therapy session. She didn't seem fazed at all by our conversation.

She had accepted the idea of Robert's reemergence as no big deal but to me it was momentous. She had tried to dispel my fears but I was not feeling anymore at ease. She seemed to think my doubts were normal but it didn't feel that way. Confronting and reliving these memories were changing me, and perhaps that is the critical information I hadn't shared with her. If she knew that I had changed over that last week, she would understand the there is more here than meets the eye.

I saw everything differently. My perfectly organized house was confusing to me. I felt lost wondering among the baskets filled with categorized contents, a planner that was eerily neat, and a lifestyle that was so efficient and orderly. My plain clothes felt constricting. These outward changes were a reflection of the conversion inside me. As I uncovered Robert's memory, I found who I was buried beneath. I saw that when Robert died I ceased to be my fun, loving care-free self. She was locked away with him and was now emerging in unison with his memory.

Apparently along with all the turmoil and memory lapses I had gained the superpower of analyzing and daydreaming to ridiculous lengths. Once again I found myself pulled from my reveling to the present where Jen and Jackie, standing by the empty bathroom shouted, "*Your Turn.*", simultaneously and enjoyed my alarmed reaction so much I found it annoying.

I took a shower, dressed, and packed my bag, but my mind was separate from my body. My arms and legs performed the activities with my thoughts vacant from the process. Outwardly I seemed fine, hollow maybe, but the turbulence inside me was roaring.

I had expressed plainly my confusion and declared my love for Robert, but the world moved about around me unchanged. More immediately Jen was futzing about with her bag and things, having left our talk behind. I had expected her to support me and not chastise my confusion, but I don't understand how she could be so unaffected.

We said good bye at the valet pickup. It wasn't particularly tearful or emotional since we were planning to see each other for the wedding. Jen gave me an extra squeeze when she hugged me. I assumed she was telling me everything would be ok. I wasn't so confident.

Jackie drove again, and we had the windows down enjoying the warmth. I rested my arm on the sill of the open window and tilted my face toward the sun. The warmth caressing my face felt good, and it kept the conversation between Jackie and me to a minimum. I couldn't bear the idea of laughing and talking petty things with her now when I felt like screaming inside. I could tell her what I had told Jen, but I was afraid her reaction would be the same. I didn't want to be told it was no big deal. Oh, you are still desperately in love with Robert and considering canceling your wedding to live out your life with his memory as your only companion, that's totally normal. It was like the person who is insane telling everyone they aren't crazy. Only for me it was the opposite. I was trying to tell them I was crazy but they wouldn't believe me.

Questions raced around my head, but I had no answers for them. I thought revealing myself to someone would help clear my muddled brain, but it was worse now.

Is this actually common? Is cold feet usually this consuming?

We turned into my development, and my stomach twisted when our house came into view. That surely didn't seem normal. I was anxious to see Troy, but due to fear not anticipation. I caught myself breathing short quick breaths and forced myself to slow them down. I concentrated on my even breathing as I grabbed my bag and hugged Jackie.

"You ok?" She looked at me quizzically.

"Just tired I guess." I answered steadily.

"I know. Me, too. The couch is sounding really good right now." She laughed.

I heard her car screech down the road as I touched the door

knob. My stomach twisted tighter. I walked into the kitchen and took it in. The counters were lined with the essentials only. The coffee pot and toaster oven were butted up to the wall. The knife set his parents had gotten us as an early wedding present sat on the adjacent counter. The organizer had spare keys hanging on the hooks. The dining room table was cleared.

Before I had been comforted by the neatness, but now it felt empty. I didn't feel a connection, though it looked familiar.

Troy wasn't home, and the couch really did sound good, so I parked my bag next to the washer. Figured I could deal with that later, or not, whatever. I grabbed the folded blanket from its home on the back of the couch and turned the TV on while I plopped horizontally. I covered every inch of myself with the blanket, toes to neck. I looked like a caterpillar in a cocoon. I scanned through the TV movies and picked something sappy. I wasn't too concerned with what was playing sure that I would be drifting aimlessly amidst my muddled thoughts in no time.

I was still trying to grasp Jen's excuses for why I was experiencing all this confusion. I never would have guessed she would respond like that. I was still surprised at her assurance that this was a normal process. I hadn't thought to ask her if she had gone through something similar before she married Andy. Perhaps that is why she was so confident that my confusion was typical.

But is her marriage comparable to what Robert and I would have had? I hate to sound pompous, but I didn't think so. It is hard for me to say that as an outside observer, but I just don't feel that

155

their love radiated the way ours did.

On the other hand, she loves him and looks forward to spending the rest of her life with him. I know she does. I can here the sincerity in her words when she talks about him. This could be me. Actually this will be me in a week, if I let it.

I thought I already made this decision when I said yes to Troy a year ago. I need to look at this differently. I love Troy. I like taking care of him, making his lunch and coffee and such. We rarely fight. We enjoy movies and going to the beach. We are comfortable around each other. He knows I love Robert still, at least if Jen is right. Why shouldn't I marry him?

Robert is not coming back. I know that. I surfaced from that suffocating agony years ago, and Troy was holding my hand while I did it. I have been talking about all this transformation within me. So what if I want to wear converse and don't care for my house being perfect anymore. I am pretty sure those are changes Troy will be willing to accept.

I chuckled when I thought of the classic break up line: It isn't you it's me. Seriously though why break up over that? If it is me, I can fix it. I can change myself so I am happier with who I am. That would be easier than the problem being him. Why should Troy suffer because I am having an extremely early bout of mid life crisis? Maybe this *was* just an unusually intense case of cold feet. I should just let my house be a pig sty, wear my hair in eight buns, and call it a day.

I felt the knot in my stomach release and was smiling to

myself when I heard Troy open the door. He peered into the living room and took in my shape wrapped totally with the blanket and grinned.

"Not feeling so hot, huh?" He teased, imagining I was hung over. He assumes that just because he has to get sloshed to party means I do also.

"I'm just being lazy. Thank you for the surprise breakfast. That was nice."

"Yup. Just wanted to show Jackie what she missed out on." He alluded to the fact that forever ago he dated her for a split second.

"Very funny. Wanna watch a movie?" I asked. He looked up on the screen, and a cheesy romance scene was failing to steam it up.

"Nah, I'm good."

"I didn't mean this. Let's watch something else. You pick." I offered. He didn't answer.

"Pick now or forever hold your peace." As the words tumbled out the double meaning kicked me. How poignant my subconscious was. I mentally rolled my eyes to myself while he opened the closet and perused our movie library. He stood before the stacks of our old VHS movies just staring.

"Seriously, pick whatever you want. I don't care." I offered.

"Uhh…alright. How about a Bond film?" He looked at me for approval.

"Ooh. Perfect. Let's watch an early one." For a Christmas

present one year Troy had bought me the entire collection of Bond movies.

"I was thinking more like Casino Royale."

"Oh. Yea. I love the chase scene in the beginning."

While he got the movie on and ready, I grabbed the fluffy down comforter off our bed and brought it to the couch. It immediately upped the coziness level and simultaneously cured my ailment of always being cold.

"You want wine?" He called from the kitchen.

"Definitely."

We were side by side on the couch, covered to our chins with the poofy comforter while our red wine glasses rested on the coffee table. It was a classic night in set up and I saw how easy we were together. We flowed in sync so effortlessly. We were comfortable and could coexist with minimal effort.

He reached for my hand beneath the blanket, and we intertwined our fingers.

I could see what Jen was talking about. I did love Troy. He took care of me, and I took care of him. We were secure in our routine, lives, and future plans. Why had I thought that was so inadequate before? I had so much to be thankful for within him and us. Ever since I had dreamt of Robert I had not been able to get him off my conscience and was constantly comparing him to Troy. How wrong that seemed now. It isn't fair to expect Troy to live up to my idolized memory of Robert. It seems to me that once someone dies they embody an angelic notion, and no living person could compete

158

with that. At least in Robert's case. I explained to myself that I wasn't settling for Troy. He was merely a different choice.

We sipped our wine, and our shoulders pressed together as we both leaned toward one another. We commented on the movie. Probably the same comments we made last time. It was nice. There was a warmth and comfort that accompanied our predictability. The credits started rolling.

"Can you handle a second?" He arched his eyebrow and mock challenged me.

"I can if you can. You're bound to fall asleep before me. It's practically a mathematical certainty. It always happens that way." I teased.

"We'll see about that. You get the movie. I'll get the wine." We made all the necessary adjustments as we transitioned into phase two of movie night. I went for the easy follow up and put in the newest Bond. Why mess with what works.

I was plopping back onto the couch when he came back in holding our full glasses of wine and sucking on a lollipop. "What's that?" I pointed to his mouth.

"My secret weapon. A little sugar rush to give me an edge in our competition. I'm going to prove you wrong."

"You didn't ask me if I wanted one. Are there anymore?" I was already heading toward the kitchen.

"Not any of the Blow pops, but there are some other bobo brand gum lollipops in the junk drawer."

I pulled the bottom drawer next to the dishwasher out and

shuffled a few miscellaneous items around before I saw them. I popped it into my mouth.

"Ugh. This is not nearly as good. Give me yours." I shouted from the kitchen.

"No way." He was smiling, I could hear it in his voice.

I sat back on the couch, but not right next to him, pretending I was annoyed he wouldn't trade. We were watching the movie when I heard crunching coming from his side of the couch. I looked over at him.

"Mmm this is so good. This is the best gum ever." His words and exaggerated manner felt familiar, and I flash backed to my first date with Robert when he was feigning ecstasy over the sprinkles.

I smiled at both Robert and Troy. "Whatever. You suck." And I bit down through the center of my lollipop. "This is the worst ever. The piece of gum is so tiny I can barely chew it." I concentrated for a minute. "Seriously, it keeps getting lost in my mouth."

We were both laughing. I was happy and content in that moment.

Perhaps I was just being sensitive before by trying to shelter my feelings from Troy. But if Troy knew I loved Robert, I didn't have to feel threatened by our marriage. It wasn't an attempt to erase Robert from our lives. It was a logical step in a relationship that had been smooth and grounded. I had been scared that our future would forever bury the feelings I had for Robert, but that was impossible. The memories I relived now were vivid and clear. They always would be. Time does not weather a love as passionate as ours.

It was a profound realization. Jen's reasoning did not seem so bizarre anymore. I could see now that I could let this love be a part of who I was. I didn't have to deny it or him. I felt resolve rise within me. I could love Troy, did love Troy, and would love Troy.

Without knowing it a delinquent tear welled in my eye.

The battle within me quieted for now, and I rested my head on Troy's sturdy shoulder. Troy was nudging me awake an hour or so later at the end of the movie.

"Come on you. Its over. Let's go to bed." He whispered.

I grumbled in response.

"Movie night was a hit, huh." He teased.

"Sorry."

"It's alright. Come on." He squeezed my hand and guided me from the couch into our room. I climbed into the sheets face down and nuzzled, in glad to be overcome by sleep again.

## Resolve

I woke to my alarm Monday morning. It was nice to find my thoughts were still steady and clear. I fell into my morning routine, repeating the same motions of making coffee, making lunch, showering. It didn't feel robotic. It felt easy.

I thought of Troy and me in the future, old. We would be the couple going to the same quaint shop for coffee and a paper at the same time each Saturday. When I envisioned it, it felt right, not monotonous. In the light of the morning, with my resolve set, I enjoyed looking into our future. There was a comfort that accompanied our stability and homogeny.

I yawned involuntarily and reached for the coffee to pour a second cup of my morning weakness. Troy's boots clamored onto the tile.

"Morning." My response was a silent gesture with a raised coffee cup.

"Did you save some for me?"

"I think there are a few drips left." I poured it into his to-go cup. I had my back to him and was pressing the lid on firmly. There was nothing like spilled coffee in the morning to utterly ruin a day.

He approached me from behind and gently but very seductively pressed his lips softly to my bare shoulder. I didn't tense or withdraw but I did briefly picture another set of lips touching me in a similar manner. I breathed in, forced myself back to the present, and handed him his coffee.

I planted a firm kiss on his lips in return, and it was ok. It wasn't heated or passionate, but it didn't feel like a lie either.

"Thanks, babe." He smiled and headed out the door.

I turned again and placed my hands heavily on the counter for support. I thought back to what was a long time ago but felt like mere moments. The days when Robert's death was new and painful. His ghost had haunted me incessantly. I could see him in everything and everywhere. I remember startling more than once when my mind conjured his perfect image where I had so often seen him before; at his desk waiting for me, leaning casually on the wall outside class, sitting on the side of my bed with his knees up and his eyes peering at me. His cologne that was too mature for a teenager but suited him perfectly would drift into my conscious randomly. The breeze would rustle my hair softly and I would imagine his fingertips gently grazing my neck.

It was during these days that Troy would kiss my lips, stroke my arm, or hold my hand and I would long for Robert, but that had been years ago. Sometimes I would close my eyes and let myself pretend. I could never hold onto the dream long enough though. Eventually, miraculously, those feelings did fade, and Robert was no longer a dominating element in our lives.

Now he had returned. My mind was once again playing tricks on me even while I was solid in my decision to continue to stay with and love Troy. I knew I would never find someone who had the unnerving quality of stimulating each individual cell of me like Robert. Or someone that was aware that I had a past love that strong, and was willing to accept that it wasn't him, like Troy. He was a saint to let me love him second best and be satisfied with that. I would have to hold onto him or live a life alone.

Once before I had managed to remove Robert from my daily thoughts. I pushed him farther and farther into the recesses of my mind. Once I had buried him deep within me I had never allowed myself to revisit his memory until now. I had intensely feared the agonizing process I would have to endure as a result of my weakness.

Now, I would learn to incorporate his memory into our lives because I could not handle erasing him this time. I had to devise a way to let him be a part of me but not to take over me because there was no other option. I could not hide it all away again. I didn't want to lose myself in the process. I can do this. I can be me, remember Robert, and love Troy simultaneously. I had a happy and stable future to look forward to. I did wonder why it was necessary for me to continually remind myself that I could do it. Was I affirming my belief, or trying to convince myself it was truth?

I was at my desk later, school had been dismissed, and I was reviewing a quiz I had given that morning when my cell phone began to vibrate. I immediately grabbed it and answered the call before it went from vibrating to singing my ring tone.

"Hello" I hadn't even looked at the name.

"Hey, Babe. What's going on?" Troy answered.

"Nothing." I answered bored. "Just grading."

"Ok. I won't keep you. Just checking in."

"Aww. That's sweet. You were thinking of me?"

"Thinking of you, please. Don't flatter yourself." He teased. "My stomach was thinking of dinner actually. You have something planned?"

"Not really. Did your stomach have something particular in mind?" I joked.

"As long as there is meat in the recipe, I'll be good with it…"

I closed my eyes and half listened while I pictured what ingredients we had to make dinner.

"…and so we grabbed" I was catching pieces of what he was saying. It was definitely work related.

I think there are a couple pieces of rockfish in the freezer, and I could thaw them fast enough for dinner to be on time. Troy had caught them one afternoon at the lake down the road. I started to picture him fishing that day, but Robert's image overpowered my thoughts.

My feet were resting on the cool rocks, and water was rippling across them as it continued down stream. He was standing in the center of the calf-deep water, somehow managing to make a vest of fly fishing lures and matching hat look adorable.

"You know you could do for fly fishing what Tiger Woods did for golf." I said

"I don't think Nike sponsors fly fisherman." Robert teased.

"Shut up. You know what I mean." We didn't talk about him being black and me being white often. We didn't avoid it by any means. It just simply did not matter. At least not to us.

"You think there is a quiet passion amidst black teenagers to be fisherman and they just need someone as skillful, handsome, and cool as me to usher in a new era?"

"Never mind." I said.


"Never mind, you aren't listening anyway. I think I'll go to a strip club and get a burger." Troy said testing my attention.

"What? Stop. I started thinking about dinner. Sorry. I'm going to thaw out that fish for tonight."

"Mmm. Frozen fish." He was being sarcastic. I guess it was a trait I was drawn to in men.

"You're a pain in the ass. I have to go. Bye."

Later I was checking out at the grocery store when my phone

started singing. I let it go to voicemail while I paid. I was walking across the parking lot and digging helplessly in my purse. I knew my phone was in there because I heard it blaring in the grocery store, but now it seemed to have vanished into thin air. Aha, I felt the edge and plunged my hand deeper snatching it up.

I played the message.

"Hey. It's me  You forgot to remind me." It was Troy, and he seemed annoyed. Why I had to remind him about every detail of his life was beyond me. Especially when I am planning a wedding and honeymoon too. I can't be expected to know and remind every one of everything.

"I have to pick up my tux tonight." This abruptly changed my train of thought; my stride stuttered. His words felt like a threat to my resolve.

Completely involuntarily my body tightened and reacted to his words that confirmed we were in the final days before our wedding. I had thought about Troy and me a lot lately. Actually I had thought about Troy, Robert, and me a lot lately but I hadn't thought too much about the wedding beyond making necessary reservations and confirmations.

It was in three days.

I continued through the parking lot, climbed in the car, and mechanically put it in gear. Next thing I knew I pulled into the driveway and realized I didn't remember how I had gotten there. I checked my rearview mirror to make sure there wasn't a police car or a pile up behind me. It looked clear enough.

My mind returned to Troy's voice message and the wedding on the horizon. I wondered for what must have been the millionth time if the inklings and constant barrage of flashbacks were normal. What if it didn't get better and in fifty years I was still haunted by apparitions of Robert multiple times a day. It was like our history was catalogued so that at a moments notice a past scene could overwhelm my train of thought. Just below the surface of my conscious was a deep ocean filled from the days of a former life. The memories were like streaming media poised to emerge whenever a situation triggered something slightly recognizable. I reached for the car door handle; It seemed the path of destruction may be ahead and not behind me.

I walked into the house and began prepping dinner. I wanted to grill the fish, so I was going to wait for Robert to get home so he could turn on the grill.

Shit. I meant I was going to wait for Troy to get home so he could turn on the grill.

I got out my book but as was common lately, found I couldn't concentrate on the text. The words blurred into alphabet soup, and my mind went blank. I didn't think of Robert or Troy or the wedding. I shut my mind down and vegetated. I was mentally and emotionally spent. I didn't want to read, watch TV, or think.

I decided to lace my sneakers and numb my brain with loud music and a quick run before dinner. I started out of the driveway with an easy pace. I thought I could head down the road and circle around the main cluster of houses in the center of our development and still have time for a quick rinse before Troy got home. My run was smooth and effortless. I pushed myself a little harder and then spontaneously took the turn out to the main road. I felt like I could run for hours without tiring. I forced my feet faster still but didn't feel winded. My arms paced, matching the speed of my legs. I streamed past trees and houses. I thought of nothing but my feet pounding the pavement and the steady rhythm of my breathing. Eventually my legs started to burn and my chest tightened. I had finally fatigued myself enough and noted the sweat on my tank top, evidence of a satisfying run. I crossed the street, reversed my direction, and fell into a slow jog.

The thoughts I had managed to block out for a brief period of time by immersing myself with the mechanics of running began seeping in. I pictured myself teetering, knowing the next day would determine much of the remainder of my life. I could continue down this path that was so seamlessly laid out before me and marry Troy, or I could put an end to what recently felt like a charade. It was now or never. I had to decide. There was no more time.

Suddenly I had a creeping feeling that someone was watching me. Paranoia swept over me. I kept up my jog and firmly faced forward, refusing to acknowledge their presence. I felt the motion of the car, a short distance back, slow to a crawl as it pulled up alongside me. I looked over while I mentally prepared to angle my feet if necessary to swiftly change direction and veer away from

169

the potential attacker.

But I recognized the face immediately and relief washed over me. All of this turmoil was putting me on edge. If I wasn't more careful I might end up in an insane asylum. I seriously had feared Troy was a kidnapper or worse. He beamed at me and pointed to his occupied passenger seat. A clean black garment bag was filling it up. It seemed he had taken care to lay it so there wasn't any crinkling of the bag or its contents.

"Fits perfect." He smile was warm and genuine, and it made me want to smile.

"Good." I smiled in response.

"Alright, just wanted to tell you real quick. I'll see you at home."

"K."

"You look sexy by the way." He smiled and sped off.

I shook my head slightly enjoying the compliment. I saw myself on the precipice again and continued for now in the direction of the house.

Troy waved with his arm extended from the deck as I approached the driveway.

"Hey. I just put the fish on. You gonna jump in the shower?"

"Yea. I'll just be a minute." I soaped and rinsed off real quick just enough to remove the sweat fragrance from my skin. I put on a favorite pair of grey sweatpants and a thrift store vintage find, a Smurfs tee shirt. I was tying my second braid with an elastic when I walked into the kitchen and paused.

Troy had plates, napkins, and utensils stacked in a pile and was carrying them onto the deck. Eating outside with the warm breeze and the sun setting made me feel a little under dressed for dinner at my own house. The setting and set up was serene, but I felt out of place; this felt different, he felt different to me. I couldn't figure out what it was. It was like he was trying to impress me which felt awkward for some reason. Perhaps because I was unsure that I still wanted to be the object of his affection.

Dinner was quiet. Not uncomfortable, though chewing did seem to fill an inordinate amount of dead air. We ate our dinners slower than usual. Maybe it was because we were enjoying the nice evening, or maybe it wasn't.

Regardless of the circumstance I made myself be present. I did not want my thoughts clouded as they had been. It wasn't fair to Troy. I needed to give us a chance, and how could I possibly do that when I was constantly throwing myself full force at one resolution after another? Either I was determined to be with him or ready to sacrifice his love to live in the past. I was always battling with who I was with Robert and now with Troy. So I gave myself to him and this evening and let it unfold without trying to discover a hidden solution. I allowed myself to surrender to the fact that I had no idea what the right decision was.

Though, I would have gladly welcomed some sort of sign to tell me what I should do. I wasn't having any luck trying to find it on my own. Dinner and the evening concluded without any sign from God or the heavens. Damn it. I wasn't surprised, just a bit disappointed. It would have been so much simpler if a voice broke through the clouds while we ate dinner and firmly stated that I was destined to be the creepy old cat lady that lived alone pining over her first love.

I probably would have been so relieved to know what to do that I would have dropped my fork on the plate and said "See Ya." to Troy. I would have been off the hook too. Troy would have to take up his grievances with God and not me because I was just following orders.

Later I climbed into bed and quickly recapped our evening in my head. It was a nice night, uneventful but not boring. As I already knew, we were easy together, comfortable. I closed my eyes and felt the familiar swirling within my brain start to rev. And in an instant the storm was stunted.

His warm hand felt rough against the smoothness of my lower back as he began to caress me. A cold tingle shot from his touch and rippled throughout my body. It wasn't pleasure. It was a system shock. My earlier indecisiveness sped into high gear. Thoughts were flying around my brain so fast I couldn't contemplate any of them. His fingers were hot to my cool skin. The difference was not welcome, it was uncomfortable. My brain was clouded with panic. My neck and shoulders tensed, and my body lay still beneath his hands.

My thoughts flashed to Robert, and immediately I felt guilty for the transgression. It was one thing to love him but another to think of him during intimate times with Troy. Or possibly I was so intensely screwed up that the guilt I felt was for Robert. This is insane. I actually felt that I was betraying my dead boyfriend by loving my fiancé!

"I'm tired, honey." I said it flat and dry. I desperately hoped he did not try to convince me otherwise because I surely would not be able to speak more than a few words in a stable tone.

I felt his hand retreat and the chilling shock rescinded. I wanted to scream. I was crazy and confused. This was not normal. How could I live this life with Troy? Would Robert be ever present, polluting each thought, emotion, and action?

Where was my resolve? I had been so sure about Troy and me at one time.

I enjoyed his company. We got along well. He was good to me. But I saw clearly now that that was the extent of it. I didn't want him to be more than a platonic companion. I could be his friend but not his wife, partner, and mother of his children. I could never do that.

Weeks of confusion and indecision were clearing up. It wasn't a burning bush by any means, but the burn his touch made to my skin was sign enough. I should not and could not marry Troy. Whether he would settle for being loved second best didn't matter anymore because I couldn't allow myself to follow through with the commitment. I was sure that it had to be this way. My mind felt at peace for that brief moment when I made this final determination. Though the idea of bailing on him and our wedding was taboo, something felt completely right about it and that was how I knew this was the decision I would stick with. It was only a moment later that it dawned on me. I had resolved to rescind the words I had affirmed only a year ago when he asked me to marry him. So where did this leave me? It left me three days from a wedding I no longer wanted and had no intention of participating in.

## Return

I woke up to my alarm, like any other day and then was beset by the previous evenings happenings.

I moved through the motions of my morning routine because I didn't know what else to do. It just didn't seem fair to break off a lifetime commitment before Troy was even out of bed.

As I moved through my morning tasks, showering, dressing, and making coffee, everything was a little off. I realized when I was brushing my overly knotty hair that I had shampooed twice and had completely forgotten to use conditioner. I tugged the mass on my head relentlessly and decided it was a mild form of deserved self flagellation. I struggled to scoop the coffee grounds out of the basket and had to start over because I lost count the first time. Throughout the morning I was cussing myself silently in my head for being such a moron. Ugh. I returned the coffee pot to it's rightful place after pouring the water into the chamber for brewing and walked back through our bedroom and into the bathroom.

I suppose I was in denial about what I needed to do because I just started braiding the left side of my hair. When I was done with that I gathered another section on the right side and braided it backwards. I pulled both sections together with the rest of my hair into a messy bun at the back of my head.

Troy lumbered out of bed, plucked my bun, mumbled that is was cute, and stepped into the shower.

I let it all roll off my shoulders. I wasn't going to break up with him through the shower curtain. Which got me thinking. When was a good time to break up with your fiancé? Definitely not at the altar. I had seen enough movies to know that much for sure.

I entered the kitchen, and my eyes zeroed in on the empty coffee pot. Where was the freaking coffee? Of all the days this was not the morning for my coffee pot to crap out on me. I could hear it brewing and steam was rising from the basket. I just stood at the counter dumbfounded. I examined it closer and realized the damn coffee was brewed and hot but stuck pooling in the basket. I pulled the pot off the burner and a piece of plastic hit the counter. That can't be good. Shit. The release lever that mercifully permitted you to pour a cup in the middle of brewing by halting its flow had broken off. Shit. I clambered for something, anything that I could press onto the release to free the coffee. I grasped a butter knife, dug around for the release, and cussed as hot coffee spilled onto my hand. I felt like a drug addict who needed a hit. Eventually I managed to liberate the coffee and started sipping it with my mug in one hand and an ice pack on my burned fingers in the other.

That was when Troy walked in all harried complaining about being late and how I shouldn't have let him sleep in.

I gritted my teeth and took a big gulp. I contemplated blurting out that I was leaving him for a dead man for a brief second but then his work radio started blaring about a fire.

He grabbed the gear I had piled on the end of the counter and turned to me. Again this felt like the wrong time to break the news. It would be bad form to darken his thoughts before he risked his life in a fire. He waved in lieu of saying good bye because his coffee cup was clamped between his teeth and his arms were full.

I had taken the rest of the week off, unsure of any final wedding mishaps I might have to extinguish. The current predicament was definitely not one I had foreseen. I would have preferred to work versus deal with this. When I really considered the entirety of the situation I knew that initially it would be horrendous but eventually worthwhile.

The bottom line was I didn't want to be married to Troy, and it was better to end it sooner rather than later. I didn't want to think about the pain this was going to cause him. I did not want to hurt him, but I told myself I was saving him from a worse pain later. Even if I went through with the wedding, I knew I wouldn't last being married to him. I would have to cut our relationship off at some point, so I should do it now.

My mom called. I let it go to voicemail, not prepared yet to speak with anyone. Her message said she was going to drop the pearl earrings and necklace off to the dress shop on her way to work. Well, that is just great I thought with sarcasm. I had completely forgotten about the appointment at 10:00 today for a final fitting on my wedding gown.

I hadn't looked at my planner in the last week because my head had been so consumed with Robert, Troy, and the wedding that I wondered what else I had missed. I pulled the planner out and didn't see anything else important. I looked to the end of the week and saw where I had written: **WEDDING** in neat capitalized block letters. It could have just as easily said dentist, except it was written on a Saturday. It seemed telling that I wrote it so plainly and business like. It struck me that the turmoil that had boiled over in the last few weeks must have begun as a quiet simmer months ago when I made this annotation.

I figured I should go to the appointment. It would be heartless to tell the shop tailor that the wedding was off before I told the groom. It was 9:00 now, so I finished getting dressed and headed out the door. It would take me twenty minutes to get downtown, and I didn't know what parking would be like. Half the street was angled parking, and the opposite side was all parallel. I was completely unskilled at sliding into these spots and had no intention of attempting it today with my brain in its current state of disturb.

The dress shop was located on the main drag in Lewes. I turned onto the street and took in the familiar scene. It still looked eerily similar to when I was in high school. The shops had collectively redone their fronts last winter resulting in a clean uniform appearance and forcing a mildly fabricated feel. The street was primarily filled with the same stores; mainly jewelry, antique, and coffee shops. I reached for the vintage brass door handle to the bridal shop and allowed myself to glance toward the ice cream store at the far end of the street. It looked practically untouched from my teenage years, and I could easily picture Robert and me laughing side by side on the bench outside on our first date.

I crossed the threshold and noticed the customary ring from the bell that hung on the door was silent. I looked up and saw it was absent entirely. The women standing at the counter held the bell delicately in one hand and examined it in the light. She smiled looking at it, pleased by her work. She was pretty with her creamy cocoa colored skin accented by a chocolate brown lacy top. Her hair was cropped short and styled skillfully.

"Sparkly clean." She commented while capping the bottle of polish she had used to shine it. "Can I help you?"

Her eyes locked with mine.

It was Chandra. I hadn't seen her in years. We had never spoken after the accident that killed Robert. The fact that we both recognized each other was obvious by our simultaneous pauses.

"Uhh. Hi Chandra. Yea, I have a ten o'clock appointment for my final fitting." I explained awkwardly.

"Hey. Ok. I hadn't checked the book yet, so I didn't realize there was a fitting first thing this morning. I'm still getting used to

179

the routine around here."

"Yea, I didn't see you the last couple times. Did you just start here?"

"Yes. Three weeks ago. This way." She motioned for me to follow her, and we stepped through a curtain separating the shop from the inner workings of the store. She collected the dress as we wound between racks of clothing waiting to be picked up or fitted.

We ascended the stairs that were tucked into the left side of the spacious storage room. She led the way. I noticed the difficulty she was having trying to maneuver the swollen garment bag up the narrow staircase. We reached the top where there was a small loft that had been renovated into a single dressing room. It was large and open with a picture window at the front allowing natural light to stream in and offering a view of the main street with a large settee beneath it. The room was decorated in shades of white covering the walls, windows, and scattered chairs. The focal point was a faux crystal chandelier in the center that completed the room with a hint of opulence.

She removed the gown from its outer casing and hung it on one of the many wall hooks. She explained she would let the tailor know I was here and changing.

I felt absolutely ridiculous trying the gown on and occupying their time and effort when I had no plans to wear it. But I was here now. The comfort of my jeans and sweater were like armor, and I felt exposed in more than the literal sense as I pulled them off. I reached for the dress, pulled it over my head and zipped it up without peeking into the mirror even once.

I stood there waiting impatiently in the deathly quiet dressing room with my back to the three way mirror. My hands at my sides in fists. I heard the bell on the shop door ring and assumed Chandra was replacing it.

A few more seconds ticked slowly by before I succumbed to curiosity and turned to face myself in the mirror. I took myself in. The dress fit perfectly. The ivory gown just skimmed the carpeted floor. It rose with cleans lines to an empire cinched waist and ended with a strapless bodice. My hair was still affixed nicely to my head with the braids and bun. I could easily have been a women ready to be photographed on her wedding day. I took a couple steps forward so that I was only inches from my reflection and stared harder into the streak free mirror. I looked deep into the glassy eyes and saw evidence of the familiar spark that had been burning brighter in the last weeks. I was leaning in to examine the flame closer when there was a light rapping on the dressing room door and my body went cold.

"Ms. Warren?" I recognized the tailor's raspy voice. "There is a black man asking for you at the front desk."

Before an instant could pass, my thoughts went to Robert. I saw his face crystal clear, though it had been a while since I had been able to conjure that perfect image. It was ludicrous. He had been dead for six years but my heart swelled at the dream. In the span of one heart beat his memory filled my mind, my heart broke again; I twisted the knob and was running as though I knew he would be there. As though him coming back after six years made complete sense. As though it wasn't crazy to know in my heart that he would be there leaning on the counter with a smirk on his smooth face, hiding the deep feelings and connection beneath.

I raced down the hall, the tailor was probably staring and regarding my lack of manners and inappropriate movements, but I didn't care. Its incredible to think I was able to see the carpet, lining the way to my destiny with his memory so completely consuming my minds thoughts, but I did. Like a homing pigeon seeking its long lost resting place, always knowing the direction to home, comfort, and warmth, I flew out from the back of the shop. As I turned the corner, I inspired quick and sharp as fear began to pierce the edges of his perfect memory, threatening to consume him once again. My mind caused my feet to turn my body, though my heart was bracing to scream as reality would invariably break through. It was slow motion, I raised my head and looked straight at the glass counter, and stopped.

I stopped abruptly as my eyes adjusted from the memory that had taken over my mind of him; beautiful, young, 16, perfect skin and smile, and took in his even more perfect image because it was real. He was standing with his head examining the carpet, his posture stiff. His shoulders were broad where they met his firm arms. He looked up. His face so different with age but so much the same. The hint of him as a teenager could be seen in the roundness of his cheeks, and the gleam in his eyes. His forehead was smooth and matured, his eyebrows thick and dark. His hair shaved off as it had always been in school. He wore a white button down shirt that complimented his muscular but not bulky build. When our eyes met his familiar smirk became a massive grin that covered his face, though his eyes seemed to be hiding pain or fear or both. My heart pumped out a beat and again I was running towards him. My feet couldn't move fast enough; it seemed like an eternity, but I was finally within reach. I leapt into his arms, unable to restrain myself. He had braced his stance and held firm even with the force of my body rocketing into him. I squeezed with my arms and clawed with my fingers into his very real frame. I could feel the ripple of his muscles through his shirt as I pressed my palms up and down his back to convince myself he was there.

In his arms I was home, warm, whole, complete, and loved. A piece of my heart immediately slid back into place, and the refreshed blood shot through my body touching and instantly healing each cell of me. I was invigorated and alive in a way that I didn't know I could be. Not until that instant had I known how deep my pain actually went. Though I knew I had been incomplete I now realized I had been broken. My heart always searching for him as my mind kept me busy with trivial details. My breath steadied, my thoughts narrowed, and my eyes focused. The pressure I felt under my fingertips told me that he was real. What to say to this enigma in front of me. I opened my mouth, but my tongue was lost and confused; no words would form. I just stared into his eyes.

He breathed deep, taking me in, and kissed me formally and gently. As his warm lips pressed into my soft cheek, I lost my breath again.

I looked up at him from beneath my lashes as tears filled my eyes.

He stepped back away from me, and I instinctively grasped his back tighter, showing my unwillingness to let him move from me. He gave a smirk, lifted his hand and wiped the tears that were filling my eyes, streaming down my face and now wetting his shirt. After my vision cleared he locked his eyes with mine and said softly "I missed you."

Tears filled my eyes again as thoughts and emotions began flooding my system. Gazing at him, I was overcome with the innumerable memories, dreams, and feelings. It was too much, and I mashed my eyelids together and tried to sort through all that was coursing through me. It was as though I was dying and my life was flashing before my eyes, but of course I wasn't. Instead of my life it was all my memories of our time together that began streaming through the self inflicted darkness and then all the daydreams and fantasies of what could have been the conclusion to those early days that made my heart swell. The fantasies were altered now with his real image filling the character of the boy that I had always fit into adult roles. The circumstances that brought my real life angel back to me did not matter at the moment. I didn't care how he came to be here now.

He was waiting for a response or a word I suppose to make sure I wasn't mute. My throat was tight, and I swallowed hard against the lump that filled it. I breathed out "I can't believe you're here".

He moved those few inches back into me, and I fully melted into his embrace. I felt drawn to his warmth as a magnet to its opposite. There were so many questions, but for now I was at peace knowing that all would be well. He would take care of me as I had always envisioned, and I was content in the most remarkable way. Each second in his arms freed me from what would have been. In my mind I said a quick goodbye to the life that had been so close to being certainty. I was no longer bound to that me-the independent, head strong, stubborn, and all too often hard woman. Robert would expect that I rely on him, and he would make everything right. I would be the one leaning upon his shoulder. Simultaneously we pressed together tighter before we released each other for the first time since I had turned the corner.

I smiled up at him as he slid his hand down my arm and grasped my hand.

"You really are here." I managed to stutter out as I fumbled my feet back onto the ground after being suspended in the air while he had held me.

"Yes." He paused. "You look beautiful."

Such simple generic words, but coming from his mouth they had the power to make me feel like I was flying. I looked down towards our clasped hands shying from the intensity in his voice and saw that I was still garbed in the wedding gown. Where I had felt ridiculous before now I felt ashamed. He was looking at me also but didn't appear upset by the dress. How much did he know?

Questions began speeding through my brain, and his voice cut through.

"Can we talk?" Robert said in his velvet tone. Forever cool and collected.

I slinked back from him and led him to the back of the store and toward the stairs, all while pressing his right arm to my body. I was ecstatic that his skin was beneath my fingers, and I touched his wrist, the wrinkled skin on the inside of his elbow, and up and down his forearm in awe. At the base of the narrow stairs I reluctantly released myself from him and carefully climbed the steps. It wasn't actually as difficult as I expected cramming the gown between the walls but then I realized Robert had gathered the extra fabric and was carrying it for me. Of course. I entered the room and turned as he took the final step. Tears were again welling in my eyes and lazily falling down my cheeks. My body was brimming with happiness, and it was spilling out in tear drops. We walked toward the window with our hands connected. Mine were dry and rough and seemed a strange but perfect complement to his powdery smooth hands.

We sat facing each other, studying each other, absorbing each trait, and committing it to memory. Seconds seemed to be ticking away in slow motion. He was patient with my incredulity; how could he not be. For all I knew I could be having a nervous breakdown. The man I had desperately missed for six long years had practically appeared out of thin air. Would he disappear with the same swiftness that he materialized? No, I didn't believe that. Now that he was before me I knew in my soul that we would get to have the life I had so desperately wanted with him.

"I, I don't understand" Our eyes locked.

He inhaled slowly. I could tell he was stalling, hesitating. Not wanting to say the words. "I am so sorry. The accident I was in. It was my fault. I was so stupid." He was getting upset so he breathed deep, collected himself and started again.

This time he started a rehearsed story that must have played in his mind countless times. "When I hung up the phone from you that last time it was because my cousin Ricky had just gotten home and he seemed desperate to talk to me. He had me go for a drive with him, and told me all about how Chandra had broken up with him. He was so hurt. I guess it had happened a few days before I flew up there. He was pissed because he had tried to get in touch with me, but I was spending every moment with you. He had wanted to talk to me and was hoping I could talk to Chandra for him before I left. We drove around all afternoon and into the evening. I tried cheering him up, but had no luck. I was feeling guilty that I hadn't returned his calls. He wanted to go to a party. I should have said no, but I didn't, and that is a mistake I have replayed in my head a thousand times over. Instead I played the best friend role and listened as he complained, cried, and carried on. I indulged him because I pitied him. We drank, and when he had relieved enough of his upset, we left. I shouldn't have been driving, but I did." He closed his eyes tight not wanting to continue.

I squeezed his hand tighter in mine encouraging him to go

on.

"I am not sure exactly what happened, but I must have missed the red light because I caught a glimpse as I looked straight up and drove beneath it. And within the same instant there was glass shattering all around us, a heavy pressure on my chest from the air bag, and then the most horrific screams coming from the darkness. I had driven us into an oncoming car and killed my cousin and an innocent family. Appallingly I was practically untouched. I was physically able to walk out of the accident, but my heart was broken as I surveyed the destruction that had occurred at my hands. I was sentenced to six years for manslaughter and I felt that the decision was justly delivered. I knew I could never come back home, to our friends, my family, and most importantly to you. I could not let the horror I caused taint anything that touched you. I entreated my family to adopt the story that I had died and hold the memorial service at our home. They were easily persuaded because a funeral seemed fitting. They mourned the loss of the life I would have had because we knew it was no longer a possibility."

I had let him run through his whole speech without so much as a wince but now the gravity of his words began to seep into me. The man before me who alone could complete my happiness was also this self described monster to others. I could not reconcile him as such in my mind.

He waited with bated breath as I absorbed all that he had laid before me. Strangely, I felt only sadness for him. The picture of him standing before the death, accident, and debris he had caused hurt me for him. I saw him standing alone in the darkness, just a scared boy who had made a mistake. "That's horrible."

He winced at my words. "I know. I am." He lamented.

He had misunderstood me.

"Robert, stop." He looked at me, puzzled. He saw himself as a monster and thought I would too. "You made a tragic mistake, but you are not a monster."

"I hate what I did to that family, my cousin, me, and us." He spit out his words. I could tell the burden was still heavy on him, as though the accident had been yesterday and not years ago. Now it was his turn to cry; where mine had been tears of happiness, his were full of despair.

"I would have stood by you. I could have been there for you." Did he think I was weak or shallow? Why would he not let me be to him what he always was to me?

"I knew that you would, which is why I didn't give you the option. I was meant to care for you not the other way around."

*Aahh*-I stifled my shout. I was angry at him. I was always completely willing to let him watch out and protect me, but why would he not let me reciprocate?

"That's not fair. How could you presume that it would be better for you to stay away? You should have let me decide! You think I would have rather wandered lost, in search of something I believed gone forever than be with you, regardless of the circumstance?" The time we had lost together began to dawn on me. It was all a waste because of his stubborn need to always protect me. Angry tears began to spill again.

"You are so selfish. You have no idea how much pain I have suffered. I never succumbed to you being really gone and have barely lived the last years of my life."

He just let me shout at him and bang my fists on his unyielding chest.

"I am not who I was when you died. I have changed. I am a different person. And here you waltz back into my life days before my wedding and proclaim your love and that you are sorry!"

"Yes." His answer exuded confidence, and I almost smiled through my anger.

I would not give in so easily though. "How could you leave me and let me think you were dead? I went to the funeral your mom had. It was horrible. I cried over you for months. I still cry over you. Your memories have haunted me all this time. It took me years to be able to get through a whole day without thinking of you." I was crying still but fury was fueling these tears. I couldn't keep up with my emotions.

"Sophia, I never went one day without thinking of you. It hurt me every minute, and you were a constant within me. It pained me to stay away knowing I was hurting you, but even more terrible was knowing that my coming back to you would be worse. Neither my presence or absence would be good for you. I was torn. I felt I would go insane searching for a way to make everything right." He responded.

"Do you know how twisted that is? It's not fair. How dare

you."

"Would you have rather me stayed gone?" He questioned. He knew my answer, which is why he delivered it in a confused tone.

"Damn you."

"That's already been done." He teased.

God, he was incredible. And I am not referring to his face or physique but his manner. His audacity in regard to our love was astounding, but best of all familiar. He knew that our unexplainable connection and unbreakable attraction was something that would remain unchanged no matter how time altered who I was or who he was. Time could pass; the earth could age; but the invisible strings linking us would never grow weak. Our love seemed to intensify even in the absence of our physical contact. It was as though it waited patiently for our reunion, strengthening until the time came when we could once again revel in its glow.

He had watched me rebel with some amusement, and now I lay spent on his chest. He wrapped his arms around me, and I calmed myself, listening to his heart, smelling his cologne. I didn't recognize the scent, but I immediately loved its smooth musk. We lay like that for a while before he suddenly but playfully scooped me with one of his arms and placed me beneath him. He put his hands on either side of me, caging me in. I felt like our bodies held a magnetic force that was pulling him to me. I teased him, feigning shock with wide eyes and a gaping mouth when I heard footsteps too late.

"Get off of her," my mom ordered, while darting across the room towards us.

I cringed as I pictured the image she must have seen when she came through the door. Me layered in a wedding gown looking startled beneath a muscular black man with his arms confining me.

"Shit." I looked at Robert and he was smirking. He would find amusement in this. I guess when your world has been destitute for as long as his nothing, not even a horrified potential future mother-in-law, can dampen that new reality.

He lifted himself off of me and helped me to a sitting position directly next to him. I sat there with my posture stark straight, eyes wide looking at my mom. I felt like a teenager who had gotten caught making out on the living room couch. Our legs were completely lined together, and I could feel his presence through the silk and crinoline.

She stood, elbows cocked out with her hands on her hips, and I saw the jewelry bag in her right hand. She must have run late bringing the pearl earrings and necklace for me. She glared at me and then Robert, back to me. She was obviously confused.

I looked over at Robert, and he was failing at his attempts to stifle a smile. It made me want to smack him, he was not helping our predicament. But it made me want to giggle a little too. What a preposterous situation.

"Annasophia." It was always a bad sign when she used my full name "What is going on here?"

"Well, Mom…this is Robert." I put my hand up and

gestured in his direction.

She looked at him skeptically, but I could tell she started to recognize him. The hard lines at her pursed mouth softened.

"Hi, Mrs. Warren. It's been a while." I rolled my eyes at him. He was so unaffected.

"Mom, it's a long story." I pulled her by the arm across the room over to the mirrors. Robert moved like he was going to get up but I didn't want him leaving my sight. I put one finger up, signaling for him to sit still.

He obliged.

She helped me out of my gown behind a curtain while I told her everything he had told me. As I was retelling the story a few questions came to mind that I made a mental note to ask him later when we were alone. For my mom's part I was impressed. She listened without interruption or question until the end.

"What does this mean Sophia?" She asked in a soft tone.

I shrugged. Robert and I hadn't really discussed the details. We really hadn't had a chance to discuss anything at all.

"What does this mean Sophia?" She pressed.

I was studying my feet. I could not bring myself to look at her. Robert here in the same room was a dream come true, but what brought me sheer joy would have the opposite effect on Troy. And what was it going to do to my mom? I didn't want to hurt her or Troy or Robert. I was cowering as I considered all the pain I would be inflicting. Could I live with myself? What Robert had done was unintentional and a mistake, but I would be consciously and willingly choosing to hurt family and friends. I can't believe it was just hours ago that I had resolved to call off the wedding with Troy. But not marrying him and running off with Robert were two totally different situations. If I was simply canceling the wedding, I would be a victim also, but in this new scenario, I was clearly the villain.

Did I want to be a monster and a villain?

No. What I wanted to do was physically vomit.

I could feel Robert fidgeting in his seat, probably because of my silence. I am sure he would have been glad to answer for me.

Why did life have to be so complicated?

## One Year Later

I hold myself supremely blest-blest beyond what language can express; because I am my husband's life as fully as he is mine.

-Jane Eyre

Life

I was sitting at *our* table in *our* diner gripping the white porcelain coffee cup that was getting dangerously low already. Fortunately our waitress new my dependence on the steamy drug and provided me my own carafe to occupy the space directly to my left. I tapped the side of the mug with my right hand and could hear the clink as my wedding ring knocked into it. The ring felt awkward and heavy there even after all this time. It was taking me longer than I thought was normal to get used to its presence. The size surely had something to do with it. Not that the stone was offensively huge it just felt like more than necessary. But he had insisted.

It had been a compromise of sorts. After the upheaval surrounding the original wedding plans I couldn't see planning it all again.  The idea of tons of phone calls, attending an array of appointments, and arranging countless details was not in the slightest bit appealing.  He was so jubilant to be getting married that he had swore I would have more than enough help but I was over the whole idea by that time.  He was understanding with the wedding and agreed on a simple ceremony performed by a family friend.  He refused to give in when it came to the ring though especially after he watched my face light up when I saw it.

I slurped another drink of coffee and surveyed the old fashioned style diner.  I took comfort in that it had barely changed in the last seven years when I first came here.  The booths were still upholstered with maroon vinyl, circular stools lined the counter which stretched almost the entire width and were topped with individual glass cake stands displaying homemade desserts.

I saw him coming back toward our table, newspaper in hand.  He was already reaching in to separate out the real estate section.  It was our Sunday morning ritual.  He would peruse the land and homes for sale meticulously trying to find one that would be perfect for us while I flipped through the rest.

I poured my second cup of coffee readying myself to read the paper while he slid into the seat across from me.

"Is the carafe empty yet?  You want me to ask for another?"  His voice eased into me and I forgot about the heaviness of my right hand.  His tone was like warm honey to a sore throat.  We had only sat down in the last ten minutes.  There was no possibility the carafe could be empty.

I stared at him pretending to be annoyed but really enjoying the attention. Robert's powdery black skin was without a blemish. His build was still firm and strong without appearing bulky. His eyes were wide and carried a softness when he looked at me. I still felt like a teenager when we got caught up staring at each other this way.

"Too early for conversation?" He continued to tease breaking from my gaze.

He was going to keep on me until a replied with some sort of quip. I knew well from previous experience. My mind was working in slow motion though because I hadn't yet polished a pot. It was like trying to turn gears that still needed a lot more oil. He was opening his mouth to spew another undoubtedly sarcastic remark so I halted him by giving him the finger.

He actually was surprised by it because generally I withheld that level of crudeness in public.

"You are desecrating that sanctity of your ring hand with a gesture that nasty." He remarked sarcastically.

"Can we please keep the conversation to a minimum until I have had a few more cups? The whole point of me wanting the newspaper is so you will have mercy and shut your trap for a few minutes." I said snidely.

"Oh. All this time I had misunderstood your intentions. I was under the impression you wanted me to scour the paper so we could buy a place to live instead of spending our days in the hole of an apartment we call home."

I just glared, willing him to be quiet.

With a smirk and a single chuckle he finally surrendered. He set to his task examining each bit of his claimed section of the newspaper. We had been trying to find common ground but had been unsuccessful thus far when trying to agree on land or a house. We both wanted a home with a lot of character but that was really the extent of our common interests.

I wanted a place out in the country, quiet, with land and trees while he would prefer a home in one of those development/towns where we could walk and bike to our destinations. It had resulted in a fair amount of contention so he ended up looking at the paper religiously every Sunday.

He graciously remained quiet while I finished the carafe and when he saw the last drips fall into my cup he immediately signaled the waitress for another. This was also her clue that we were ready to order our breakfast.

While we waited for my pancakes and his eggs he laid the paper down on the table so I could read it. He pointed to his favorites sharing little tidbits of each to defend his choices.

"This one is my favorite of the week, it's a land home package. The lot is in a cul-de-sac so there is a little extra land and there are three restaurants, a salon, a pharmacy, and a gym." He offered.

"But no dollar general or thrift store. Where would I be without my favorite spots?" I asked him.

"Soph, the dollar store is full of crap and you could have

your own thrift store the way you cycle through their clothes."

"Just because you have a love affair with Polo doesn't mean that all other clothing is sub par." I kidded defensively.

"Classic never goes out of style. I still have shirts in my closet from high school. You know what we should do is designate a room for you to keep your clothes in instead of donating them back to the thrift store. That way you can shop at your own convenience. If it would make you happy I will charge you for them again and donate the proceeds." He was always giving me a hard time but like me he was driving a ten year old car and his running sneakers were in tatters. It wasn't that we didn't want to spend money and it definitely wasn't that we didn't have money. We just didn't feel the need to spend money simply because it was available.

"Now stop and look at this one with me please." He begged.

I obliged pouring over the picture. It was a nice set up but I could never call this place home in its cookie cutter development. Each house a shade of beige with a manicured front lawn.

"It's kind of creepy I think. It's like they are pulling us in."

"You are incorrigible"

In a monotone voice I said "Please, come live here. We have everything you need. You will never have to leave."

He looked at me and I could see annoyance tighten his eyes.

"It's like a modern day Hotel California" I continued.

To this he threw his hands up. "Fine, we will just live in a crappy apartment until we are old and grey. One of us will end up falling down the stairs with our walkers and then we'll end up in some dirty dingy retirement home."

"Sounds like a plan." I agreed.

"Why do you have to be so stubborn? I have showed you fifteen houses but you won't give an inch."

"Robert, you have showed me different homes with the same exact set up. They could easily have all been done by the same designer. It's not the location that's the problem."

Our food arrived just in time before our voices raised above the polite level and stares started heading our way. We were like this a lot. We started out calm and collected and then spiraled into the same fight. But the argument was as much a ritual as the coffee and newspaper.

This simple routine was what I would consider bliss. I was at peace here with him. We weren't a Norman Rockwell all the time but I didn't want to be. Robert was worth loving for me and that meant he was worth fighting with and for. Things hadn't always been smooth over the last twelve months. There had been quite a few bumps in the road especially early on but we took it all in stride and most importantly side by side. Our lives were in harmony and had been since he walked back into my life one year ago.


I reminisced to that day when he had stepped back into my life. I was standing before my mom.

My face was feeling hot and my stomach was still twisting. I sighed heavily. "It means there isn't going to be a wedding. I am sorry Mom."

I didn't know what I expected to happen when I uttered those words but to my delight the world did not come crashing down on my head so that seemed an encouraging sign. I looked up at her timidly.

Her face was blank.

"I am not sure what is going through your mind with this new revelation but don't worry about the wedding. I will take care of it. I promise. Even if I have to pay you in installments. This was my mistake and I will fix it." I was gushing at her when she put her hand up to stop me.

"Sophia, I can't imagine what you are going through right now but are you sure that this is what you want?" She questioned.

When she put it in those words the question was easy to answer. "Without a doubt Robert is who I want."

She studied my face not completely convinced.

"Mom I was planning to tell Troy I didn't want to get married anyway. I was sure last night even before Robert came back. I just hadn't been able to do it yet." I continued.

"Oh. Well, in that case I am proud of you. I would never want you to marry and spend your life with someone you didn't truly want to be with. I would be happy to cancel ten weddings so you could marry the person that is completely right for you." She explained.

I hugged her tightly. She was amazing.

"I am hoping this will be the last cancelled wedding." Robert piped up from the back. "This isn't going to be a real life

Runaway Bride type of thing, right?"

I turned to him and as I had so many times when we were younger had the urge to stick my tongue out. Instead I smiled glad to be the target of his teasing.

Outside the shop we said bye to my mom who was still handling the news with poise. There wasn't much more to say after I told her the wedding was off. I hadn't been ready to face Troy afterwards. Not because I was upset or worried. I just didn't feel like having any other interruptions between Robert and me. As we turned a separate way from my mom he put his arm out for me to seize, and I did immediately. My feet felt light and my heart skipped. It was early evening now and dusk was just starting to settle around us. He drove out of town and I didn't ask where we were going. I knew I would have to face Troy soon but I wanted to steal a few more hours with Robert before reality set in.

The obstacles that would need to be addressed could wait a little. I held them at a distance in my mind refusing to let complications distract me in this moment. I tucked my hand under his thigh needing to be in physical contact with him.

I closed my eyes and reminisced to when I first laid eyes on him in the bridal shop. My whole body had swelled with practically every emotion on the spectrum. Fear that it would not be him when I looked up, then exhilaration when it was, and the indescribable mix of happiness, love, and contentment that settled into me as we embraced.

The reality of Robert being back had not yet collided with how my other life would respond; for now it seemed separate. His reemergence was going to profoundly effect not only my future but others as well. What brought my heart sheer joy was going to have an opposite effect on Troy. For once I was not more worried about him than myself. I was going to be the selfish one now. I would not let this quandary dampen the fact that all I ever wanted was gripping my body and heart at this very moment. I suppose the thoughts racing through my head had caused my body to tense involuntarily because Robert looked over at me.

We drove in quiet for a while until he pulled into a small coffee shop that looked deserted. We walked in and the aroma filled my nose. It was filled with dark wood and the low ceilings provided an intimate feel. There was no one in the store besides us and a teenager behind the counter with a nose ring.

"You still like coffee, right?" He asked.

"Don't say *like* around the beans they will be offended. A passionate love would be a more accurate description."

He smiled and rolled his eyes.

We sat with our cups in the far corner that was occupied by oversized upholstered chairs. We shared a seat with my legs draped over his lap. The picture of comfort.

"I hope there aren't too many wedding gifts to send back. The price of postage has gone up a lot in the last few years." He teased rubbing his hand up and down the length of my thigh.

"You are such an ass" I scoffed. "How can you kid me about

this. It's not funny!"

"Don't worry. It will all be fine." He affirmed.

"This is all so easy for you, huh."

"I wouldn't say anything about this current situation is easy but I will try to make it that way for you." I knew he meant it. I knew that he would not rest until everything was laid out right for me, for us.

"You know there are a few loopholes in your story?" I said not meeting his eyes and tracing lines on his forearm.

"Really?" He challenged.

I pulled myself away a little to face him and propped my elbows behind me on the chair's arm. "Yes. When I was telling mom your story a few questions came to mind that I took note of so I could ask."

"Like..."

"Like did you know I marrying Troy? And when did you find out? How did you know where I was? Was it Chandra?" I paused to take a breath and he put his arms up pretending to surrender.

"Ok, Ok." He smiled. "I had come back to stay with my mom two days ago. I was planning to come see you, I just hadn't figured out when. I kept waiting for the right time. But maybe that would never have happened. I was finding there is probably never a *good time* to deliver bad news." His remark resonated with me.

It was what I had been considering that morning, trying to find a good time to tell Troy it was over. My shoulders sunk a little as I realized good time or not it was going to happen soon.

"First of all nothing about you being alive is bad news." I scolded. "Secondly, Did you know I was getting married? Have you been keeping tabs on me? How did you find me?" My questions were opening new questions and I wanted answers.

"I had asked my mom and Chandra over the years about you but they never really new anything. I am sure they could have poked around more but neither had the real desire to. I even tried googling you. Frequently. But never came up with anything." He confessed. "I didn't know you were getting married until Chandra called me that morning. I can't even describe what happened inside of me when she said she had seen you and that you were still there, in the shop, trying on your wedding gown. I was in agony that you had decided to marry but elated that you hadn't yet. Next thing I knew I was walking out the door, keys in hand. I hadn't consciously decided but it was like my heart was making my body move. The rest is history I guess. Satisfied? Can we let the Spanish Inquisition rest?" He teased.

I don't know what I expected. Did I think he was going to say he had been waiting for the week of my wedding to reappear? What did it matter? He was here now. And always would be.

# Home

We finished breakfast and reluctantly returned "home" to our 600 sq. foot apartment. We had started renting it in June the week after getting married. There had been no discussion about what sort of space we wanted because we were only planning on being there for a month at the most. So at the time we hadn't cared that we would have to walk the groceries to the second floor, that there was no washer and dryer, and that it was a 35 minute drive from my school. Our plan was to buy a house near my work and move in as soon as possible so we could be well settled before the school year started in September. Unfortunately things had not panned out so well.

Being that the apartment was a temporary solution we hadn't decorated at all and were literally using plastic furniture in the dining room. It was a patio set his parents were getting rid of. We were in limbo and neither of us wanted to buy anything, do any work, or decorate in the apartment because we wanted to get out. I think we feared if we started attempting to improve the space we would end up residing here even longer. We couldn't commit to any furniture or textiles not knowing what sort of home we were going to buy. So instead we had nothing on the walls, cuddled on a worn leather couch from the thrift store, and slept on mismatched bedding. The contrast between this apartment and the town house Troy and I had shared was comical. If I had felt stifled with the order and neatness of that house than you would think I would feel free and unbounded here but that feeling had worn off five Sunday papers ago.

Robert's office is the only space we had spent time and money on. As a result It did not look like it belonged in the apartment at all. The walls were olive green with a leather painting technique applied. We had tried to do it ourselves and failed miserably. We ended up hiring a professional and it was worth the money. The mahogany desk we found antiquing one day melded beautifully with the wall color. There wasn't space for much else but he had insisted on a comfortable chair adjacent to the desk so that I could relax or read in the room with him while he worked. It was a good thing he had because we spent more time in there than all the other rooms combined aside from our bedroom.

When we walked into the apartment after breakfast I tossed my sweater onto the rumpled comforter on our bed and took the two steps from our door into his office. He was already behind his desk as I plopped into my chair. I picked up a manila folder he had tossed at the front of his desk while digging in the drawer for something.

I considered the image in my hands.

A tear. Paused in time, resting on the leathery pale skin of an old man. It was swollen with years of regret and sorrow. It laid beneath a glassy eye that showed sadness and loss as simply as a mirror shows a reflection. You couldn't know for sure what the cause leading to the encapsulated pain was by examining the picture but you could get lost wondering. I held the unedited rough cut in my hands and pondered the man's life. What event or circumstance had led him to such woe? The image was simple yet profound. It moved me each time I studied it. I was fingering the familiar worn edge when Robert's firm hand cupped my shoulder. I reached up and patted it.

"Why do you torture yourself with that picture?" He questioned.

"Nothing you made could torture. Its human. It's beautiful." I responded while laying it back in his portfolio and wiping my moistened eyes.

Robert had taken a photography class in prison on a whim. He credits me for the motivation though I was never a photographer. I had only ever considered myself that annoying person halting the fun to capture the moment.

The class was rudimentary and utilized outdated cameras and equipment because that was what was available. In and age when practically all images are taken digitally and enhanced via computer he had been taught to capture pictures on 35 mm film and develop them in a dark room. Robert was provided minimal education and aged equipment but his raw images picked up the essence of whatever he was spotlighting. His teacher a fellow inmate quickly recognized his natural talent and greatly encouraged him. Robert had minimal access to subjects outside the prison so he focused on anything and everything inside its walls. His photos were generally macro-photography of worn hands, tired eyes, and an array of facial expressions.

He told me once how initially he received a fair share of slack for toting his camera all the time. He didn't elaborate on what he meant by slack, he didn't elaborate on much of anything when it came to the years he spent there. The few brief times he did share stories, which always connected to his pictures, I could feel his despair. It didn't take long for the prisoners to accept his hobby. So many of them had been forgotten not only by society but also family and friends that they were appreciative of his attention. His pictures became infamous among the prison population and then the guards. After sometime his notoriety spread to the local paper where a full page was dedicated to his art. That was how he made his first sale as an artist. That purchase led to others as his work spread through the higher society circles.

"I haven't looked through those in a long time." Robert said it so quietly I wondered if he had meant it for my ears. He picked up the entire portfolio sat in our oversized leather chair and patted his leg. I sat across his lap making a desk of sorts for the folder and we slowly weeded through the images. He didn't say anything. Didn't tell me the story about the subject or the time he took the picture. He gave each image a few moments consideration and went to the next without any reaction I could detect. When we had looked over each one at his measured pace he closed the stained manila sleeve, sighed, and disconnected himself from all the emotions inherent in the pictures.

"Let's go get ice cream." He said flatly. It was ten in the morning on a Sunday and it was raining. Ice cream did not sound tempting but I knew it would pull him from the melancholy mood the pictures had caused.

"Ok, but I want the good stuff. We are going into Lewes."

"Perfect." He smiled.

He was guiding me to the car with his hand at the small of my back when he quickened his step to open the door for me. It had taken me awhile to get used to all his gentlemanly gestures again but now it was second nature to pause and allow him to take care of me.


It ended up being warmer and sunnier in Lewes so after ordering our ice cream we walked around town eating our cones. After completing the loop around the main street we headed down into the residential area where old houses lined the streets. Some were in need of renovation with damaged siding, empty gardens, and sagging roofs. It was still easy to see the potential each one held especially when you encountered a home that had been redone in the last few years.  There was one in particular that I was fond of and he made a point to move us in its direction.  It was a small cream cottage with white shutters and a garden that might look overgrown at a glance but more careful examination proved the height and spread of the plants was actually meticulously planned.  Whenever I gazed at this house I imagined the couple's life inside its walls.  I saw them eating croissants with coffee at an antique wooden table that was being kissed by the sun shining in through the window.  I could easily fill the couple with Robert's and I's faces and took pleasure in the idea of us growing old in this house together.  It felt like home even though I had never been inside.

"I would love to live there." I sighed.

"It *is* beautiful but you have never even been inside." he challenged.

"I know.  I can just feel it.  You find me something like that and I will move us into it myself."

"Is that a promise?  I was starting to wondering if you had some freaky attachment to the apartment's outdated cabinets and bathroom fixtures."

"Hmm.  It will be difficult giving up the pink toilet." I laughed.  I had finished my cone and was hugging his arm with both of mine while we headed up the last leg of our walk when we spotted a for sale sign.  It was spray painted onto a piece of plywood and leaning on a stack of tires.  We looked up and took in the house which was quaint and full of character.  It was the color of coffee and the barn style wooden shutters were painted black.  The siding was vinyl but made to look like cedar shingles.  It had two rows of windows but was shorter than newer two story homes.  The most interesting aspect was the roof of a separate building that was partially hidden by trees.

"Oh my gosh Robert."  The next moment he was leading me up the brick walkway to the front door that had been painted a bright red.  We made an offer that day.  Unfortunately the inside of the home did not match the composed picture the outside had provided. It was going to take a lot of time and money to update the interior to our satisfaction.

## Done

"I can't pick anything else out tonight. I am done." I threw the swatches of granite samples onto the outdoor patio table almost tipping it over. The place was hideous. The outdated interior we initially joked about was now a daily eye sore and we needed to get out. But first we had to completely renovate the interior of our future home.

It had been three weeks since we first saw it and all we had done since was stare at colors, textures, knobs, lights, counters, and every other minuscule detail that fills a house. I hadn't realized how many choices there would be when we started the renovating process. Everything from bathtubs to door hinges had to be chosen. Along with decorating we had decided to contract the renovators ourselves, which meant lots of phone calls and nagging. I was exhausted, spent, and annoyed. Robert had offered to have a designer help us but I knew he really wanted us to do it together. We were planning on living in this house for the rest of our lives and he wanted it to be exactly right. The problem was in the meantime we were debating each choice like it was a crucial decision like whether we had nickel or chrome faucets would impact world peace.

"Ok." He said calmly and that annoyed me. Like he was trying to placate me. "Let's just finalize our choice for the kitchen counters tonight and leave it at that."

"Uhhh. No, I AM DONE!" I enunciated.

He just held his face firm like a smile was going to burst forth and he was trying desperately to hold his composure.

I don't know what got into me sometimes but tonight I just wanted to squeeze him and not in a passionate way. I stood up and stormed into our room. I threw myself onto the bed face buried in the pillow. I lay there for a few moments and felt ridiculous. My caring, loving, and patient husband had bought the house I fell in love with at first sight no questions asked and was now by my side helping me redo the interior so it would be perfect and I was acting like a spoiled brat throwing a hissy fit. I was too embarrassed to apologize and besides he would undoubtedly enjoy that more than I would like anyway so I lay stubbornly on his side of the bed smelling him on his pillow. A couple minutes later I turned over stared at the ceiling and resolved to get up and go back to him with my proverbial tail between my legs.

Before I could he came in and stood at the foot of the bed.

"You better?" He asked.

I nodded my response.

He stepped onto the bed and crawled up suspending himself above me. "If not I put all the floor tile samples on the table too so you can toss them around also?" He pressed. He would do something like that to irk me.

"I'm fine." I said staring up at him.

"Good." And he leaned down touching his nose ever so lightly to the nape of my neck and drawing his lips up to my ear. I tried to turn my face toward him for a kiss but he pushed against me with his jaw. He pulled my shirt down a little exposing my collar bone and traced his lips along its line then yanked his head back and stared at me.

"I love you even when you are crazy." He loved to tease me but he always knew when to give me a little extra tenderness to melt all my tensions away.

I pulled him down onto me and kissed his mouth deeply. Our tongues melded together and then our bodies followed suit.

The next morning I was pouring a cup of coffee when I noticed the piles of samples, decorating books, blueprints, and other renovation paraphernalia were missing. I could see the entire kitchen counter for the first time in weeks. Robert walked into the kitchen wrapped in his towel and pretended not to notice their absence. I arched both of my eyebrows at him asking silently, What is going on?

"I packaged everything up and loaded it in your car. I thought you might want someone else's opinion and didn't know if you would be interested in showing them to your mom or Jackie after school today."

"You are amazing. You know that right?" I responded. I could swear sometimes he knew me better than I knew myself.

"That's what you keep telling me."

The students had state testing this entire week which meant I wouldn't have any homework to bring home and grade so my evenings were completely free. This was the perfect opportunity to go see my mom. On lunch break I called to see if tonight worked. On a whim I tried Jackie but had to leave a voicemail when she didn't answer. I wasn't surprised she was keeping extremely busy lately, especially since she began heading up her own branch at the architecture firm. She had been promoted in the fall as supervisor of all beach home design and with resort towns lining the Delaware coast it was a lot of responsibility. I was sure she could have made more time but frankly our relationship had been strained ever since Robert came back.

She was so defensive of Troy that it began to create a wedge between us. I had tried to bridge the gap and Robert had pushed me also. I think he feared I might come to blame him for the distance in our relationship but I would never. Eventually I came to resent that even if she didn't understand or agree with my choice couldn't she at least be content that I was happy?

I closed the phone with one hand. At least I tried. I was

really looking forward to splaying everything out on my parents kitchen table and getting their opinions. It wasn't that I didn't enjoy debating and arguing over the details with Robert I just needed to break out of it for a night. We had been at each other for three weeks and it was wearing on me.

"Hey Babe! I just talked to mom and she is excited to help."

"Good. I knew she would be." He said it in an omniscient way but it didn't feel condescending at all. The reality was he knew I was reaching my boiling point and he also knew exactly how to unfetter my tension.

"Yea. I am really looking forward to it. She said she would have dad make something good for dinner." I continued.

"Good. Not to change the subject away from you but..."

"Haha. I am listening."

"Some buyers in Georgia have been pressing me to come down and have a showing in their friend's new gallery. I hadn't mentioned it because I was trying to hold them off until after the renovations were done and we had moved in but since that is going to be farther off than we initially thought I was hoping to go in the next couple weeks. I wanted you to go with me but there is no way with all this going on." He was saying it almost apologetically.

"Robert, that is awesome news. They want to showcase your work. Don't worry about me, this will be great for you." I pushed. I was sure the slightest bit of hesitation from my end and he would have refused their offer. Sometimes his indulgence of me resulted in sacrifices for him and I didn't want it to be that way. I would hate to think in forty or fifty years he would regret a decision he made because he had considered my wants over his needs.

"It should only be a few days that I will actually be gone. The next few weeks are going to be crazy though because I am going to have to scramble to get all my stuff together. Plus I haven't really done anything new so I should try to have at least a couple of pieces no one has ever seen." I could tell possibilities were streaming into his head. I got off the phone with him so he could focus and channel his energies.

When I got to my parents house Dad was covered up with his favorite apron. It was an old fashioned blue and white checker pattern with stains that boasted past masterpieces. It had been the topic of many a dinner party and I think he purposely didn't wash it so he could show off the battle scars to guests. Mom had completely cleared the dining room table and it took us two trips to bring in all the stuff Robert had packed in my trunk.

"Where is Robert?" My mom asked emptying pamphlets and mini tiles onto the table.

"He isn't coming. He thought it would be good for us to take a break and get a fresh perspective on decorating ideas."

"Ahh." She said pleased by his sensitivity.

"He is going to Georgia in a couple weeks for a gallery showing." I mentioned.

"That's great. He must be excited."

"He is. I think he has been so focused elsewhere that he

forgot how much pleasure he gets from doing his photography. Just because he doesn't have to work doesn't mean he can't. You know?"

We set everything up on the table and circled around it like vultures. We stood while eating Panini sandwiches filled with goat cheese and smoked ham and we poured over it all. My mom and dad had a great time pointing out the samples that reminded them of previous apartments and homes they had lived in.

At one point my dad held up a square of brown shag carpet and waving it at my mom asked "You remember this?"

"Don't remind me." She laughed

"Eww. Seriously, you guys had shag carpet. That is horrendous. I can't believe they even put that one in here."

"Oh. Don't go there missy. You remember what your room looked like before Robert helped you repaint it."

My mouth fell open as the image of my bright orange and purple room flooded my mind. "I hold the two of you completely responsible for that." I said pointing at them. "Who let's an eight year old pick her room colors?"

"You always had very definite ideas for how you wanted things to look." My mom plucked my hair which I had done in three French braids pulled into a bun.

"Alright, Alright." I put my hands up in surrender.


The next couple weeks flew by. State testing was over which

meant many of my evenings were occupied grading short stories and long division. It worked out well though because Robert was so busy getting ready for his show that he wasn't much company anyway.

His flight was scheduled for noon so I couldn't take him to the airport. I wanted to be there to say goodbye. I pictured him holding me off the ground and us hugging and kissing like in a movie. He had gone to Georgia once before to sell a few pieces. It had been a brief trip, thankfully because I was on pins and needles the entire time. Robert could have mailed the three prints that had been chosen but for the price he was fetching he felt it more appropriate to hand deliver them.

The morning of his flight he wanted to run since he would be traveling most of the day, so we got up early together. I put on grey shorts with a light blue long sleeve shirt. My sneakers were new and I had bought the knit hat I was wearing the week before at a thrift store. Robert hadn't yet commented on the multicolored skiing cap that was topped with a pom-pom. He stepped out of the bathroom with his long board shorts on and no shirt. His chest and arm muscles were well defined and lovely to drool at.

I started walking in his direction. "I can think of another form of exercise." I said reaching onto my toes and pecking his lips.

He pulled the strings on both sides of my hat down so it practically covered my eyes. "Later. Come on nerd."

"You could at least run without a shirt. It would motivate me to keep up with you better." I teased.

223

He rolled his eyes, pulled his shirt over his head, and reached for his shoes. I made a mental note to buy him new sneakers while he was gone. I was pretty sure he'd those since high school.

We hit the road and I took in the crisp morning air. There was a bluish tint to the dawn everything felt fresh and new. I breathed to the depth of my lungs and my chest rose as it filled. It was silent outside and I focused on the sound of our feet touching down rhythmically. Running with Robert was so different from when I used to do it by myself. Before when my feet would hit the ground it was as though I was fighting with the pavement. My sneakers would strike in a malicious way. With Robert I ran content enjoying the release but not forcing it out of me as I had. I still ran with music sometimes but just as often I let my mind wander aimlessly enjoying his quiet company.

I started thinking about him leaving and told myself in no time at all he would be back. I was proud that he had done so well with the photography and equally as glad that it brought him happiness. The idea of him at a desk day in and day out conjured a miserable image. He had too much inside him to merely file documents and attend meetings. Watching him take pictures over the last couple weeks, had shown me how this artistic outlet invigorated him. He had scrutinized the pictures and the ones that made his final cut always had something special about them. He had decided to focus on 2nd St. where the shops brimmed with history and character. Though they were pictures of how the street looked currently the way he developed them gave the impression they were from forty or fifty years ago. I found comfort that we could glimpse the past in his pictures, when the world seemed to be changing so fast around us. I envisioned him showing off these new images to the gallery guests and was sure they would enjoy them.

We turned at the halfway mark and started picking up the pace. My legs were beginning burn. I imagined him holding me in his arms when I picked him up at the airport and this renewed my energy. My legs were smoothing along as I thought about kissing him passionately for anyone nosy enough to watch. We still turned heads with the difference in our skin color and I actually enjoyed it a bit. A smile hinted across my face and these images were enough to power me back to the apartment door.

## Letters

I threw my keys onto the counter and slung my bag full of papers to grade next to them. Ugh. It had been a long morning. The day had dragged, I didn't have Robert at home to look forward too, and the students had been all wired from their three day weekend. I wish parents would remember that I have to deal with twenty students the next morning after they have let them stay up late and gorge on Halloween candy. I reached for the bottle of wine and my shoulders slumped when I saw there was enough for only one short glass. I opened the refrigerator and pulled out leftovers from last night's dinner.

The phone rang and you would have thought there was a bomb in my bag the way I started digging through frantically searching for it.

"Hello?" I sounded keyed up even to myself.

"Hey Babe." Warmth spread through me and I relaxed my shoulders as his voice caressed my ear. "Sorry I didn't call earlier. I figured you would be getting home around now so I just waited."

"That's ok. I did just get home actually. Everything going ok?"

"Yup. I am looking the photographs over one last time to be sure I don't want to arrange them differently."

"They are going to love them. I can't wait to talk to you after the show and hear what everyone had to say." I gushed.

"Yea, Yea. Oh, guess what? When I was at the airport I checked for any earlier flights and was able to get one for Thursday at 11:00. You think you can get out a couple hours early to come pick up your poor homesick husband?"

"Definitely. I will figure it out."

"Did you like your present?" He asked.

"What present?" I said confused.

"Oh, shoot. I think I forgot it on my desk. I meant to leave it on the counter for you."

He was still finishing his sentence while I was opening the door to his office and eyeing the small package sitting in the middle of his desk. I undid the twine and pulled the brown paper off. I ran my fingers over the worn cover and embossed letters. It was an old copy of Jane Eyre.

"You get major points for this one." I was swallowing back the lump in my throat. His thoughtfulness was unparalleled.

227

"I thought you might like it."

"You thought right." I hadn't read Jane Eyre since high school. We hung up, I gobbled dinner down, and sped through my grading. I was curled up in our oversized chair with my legs hanging over the arm reading Jane Eyre. I got consumed in her story and it was 1:00 a.m. when I finally forced myself to close it and go to bed. I climbed into the loneliness of our empty sheets and thought back to that first night Robert and I had spent together.

It was the middle of the night and we had no where we had to be. It was liberating knowing that we could be together without interruption. We could be selfish with our time and not waste one bit of it worrying about the ripple effects our reunion had. We ordered room service, talked, and reminisced. We took all night holding one another, embracing, touching, and rediscovering every inch of our compliment. It felt as though our bond had tangibly strengthened over the last few months. It was as if our proximity to one another amplified the invisible link that had connected us during his years of absence.

Before I had worried how my opposing selves would merge together? Would I cease being the head strong woman or would she somehow meld with my old self? Now I saw that I never truly was that progressive women. She was just shielding the easy, free spirited, flighty girl within. I would once again be permitted to exist as her, with Robert watching out for me. I would be carefree with each day because Robert was demanding to fulfill the role of protector.

We had been awake all night long and now with the sun rising we dressed for the day. I was looking forward to all the future mornings we would have like this. We had made a public commitment to one another that matched the commitment our souls had made so long ago. Not a flutter had stirred my stomach or heart at anytime leading up to or during our wedding. Being with Robert was effortless. He was selfless and indulging. My happiness was his priority and he lived it out as though it were a decree.

I rustled in the sheets of our shared bed and with those memories swarming in my mind I fell asleep happy and comforted the same way I had felt ever since Robert came back to me.


Wednesday afternoon I opened my car door and was struck by how messy it was. Cinnamon square crumbs littered the seat and floor, travel mugs with varying amounts of cold coffee filled the cup holders, and a brown paper bag piled full of clothes meant for the thrift store occupied the passenger seat. Robert wouldn't be able to call this evening with the gallery show so there was no reason to race home today. Instead I went to the car wash and was glad to have it scrubbed and vacuumed. At least this way he wouldn't be able to harass me about it on the way home from the airport tomorrow.

I flashed to the image of me tackling him in the airport and a smile plastered my face. I blared the music and turned left toward the side road that led to the thrift store. I should have just dropped the bag in the bin outside but I couldn't help myself. Thrift stores were tempting because you never knew what you might find. There is no other store where you can purchase a glass Waterford pitcher *and* lipstick red patented leather heels like I had a couple months ago. I wandered up and down the racks, stood before the jewelry case, and stared at the wall covered with hats, scarves, and purses. Nothing grabbed my attention until I was turning and saw Jackie pulling a black shirt off the rack to examine. She hadn't seen me and I instinctively shouted her name. She turned in my direction as I walked toward her waving.

"Hey. How are you?" I asked enthusiastically entering the aisle she was in.

"Fine. You?" She was trying to mimic my excitement but it didn't fell genuine.

"Good. Just dropping some clothes off but couldn't resist checking in to see if there was something I might want. No luck today though." I continued. "I wish we could get together sometime soon. You still staying really busy at work?"

"Oh, yeah. Pretty busy. You still working?" As she said it her gaze fell on my ring finger curled around my bag strap and I felt uncomfortable for some reason. She examined the rock and I was left feeling guilty. It wasn't as though I had flung it in her face. We didn't show off our wealth. The ring was one arena where he had been a little excessive. It did concrete the fact that we were comfortable financially.

"Yes." Of course I was still working. What the hell was that supposed to mean? Like Robert was my meal ticket. Maybe I was over doing it. I just didn't like how she was making me feel. The silence was immediately awkward.

"I'll call you sometime, ok?" I said with the enthusiasm in my voice waning.

Her shoulders eased slightly as I ended the conversation and backed away.

I suppose she was glad to get rid of me. Ugh. And I had said I would call her. Why did I always position myself to have to pursue her? I should have said for her to call me so the burden would be on her. Now I have to go through another equally awkward encounter just so she can make some lame excuse not to meet me again. I hadn't mentioned her to Robert lately and whenever he asked about her and I getting together I just repeated the excuses she had given me. I didn't want to acknowledge that if she wanted to she would have made time. It was clear now that her alluding me was purposeful and planned.

What was her problem anyway? Was she jealous? Of Robert and me? Maybe she felt that her spot in my life was challenged when he came back. I would have been glad to still confide in her though. I loved him more than myself but I still wanted to strangle him sometimes. Like last month when he washed three loads of laundry, scooped them out of the dryer, and squished them onto the couch in a massive heap. By the time I got home they were all wrinkled and I had to re-dry them. It would have been great to complain about him needing a Laundry for Dummies instruction manual or something but she was never available.

She couldn't be jealous of our money. She had plenty. And shit she drove a BMW. I still drove a freaking used up Mazda. I was looking forward to walking in the door of our crappy apartment, reading Jane Eyre, and forgetting our run in.

At school I had eaten my homemade triple decker peanut butter and jelly sandwich while the students were at lunch so I could power through grading. Now I had the whole evening to be with Jane as she moved into the Rochester Estate. I read in our oversized comfy chair because it felt like Robert was holding me. The chair arm pressed into my side and I curled into its back with my head resting on it. Robert had worked in his office so much over the last few weeks that his presence felt concentrated in the room. It was easy to picture him palms down leaning over the Mahogany desk with his head bent scrutinizing the images resolution, coloring, and clarity. I was glad he would be back tomorrow.

The apartment had felt empty without him which is practically impossible considering its minute size and the quantity of crap we had crammed in over the last few months. With the renovations coming along we had both started buying lamps, pillows, and assorted other knick knacks we wanted to have in the house and there were small piles of boxes in every corner. It must have been challenging for him to work in this cramped space. We were already planning to transform the garage in the back of the house into his artist Mecca. He would have space for displaying photos for inspection, there would be an updated dark room, and ample space for his brain to expand its ideas. The garage had originally been a barn. The walls were sturdy but the roof sagged, there was a dirt floor, and the inside was unfinished with exposed beams and walls. It had been repainted some time ago and its age really showed due to discoloration and peeling. I knew it would eventually make a beautiful space for him and it proved the house was perfect.

For the second night in a row I was reading late. It was 11:00 p.m.. I thought I might have better luck falling asleep if I read in bed so I laid down on my side with the book open. I read a few lines and realized I couldn't fall asleep with the ceiling light shining either. I padded across the hall back to his office. I needed a book light which we didn't have but I had seen him with a small light for examining points in his photos.

I surveyed his desk and rifled through the papers lining the top. Nothing. I opened the top drawer and shifted its contents around but came across only pens, paper, erasers, notes, and other miscellaneous forgettables. I went to the far left drawer and carefully sifted through. It was deep and I didn't want to miss the small light in my haste. At the very back of the drawer on the bottom a small neat pile of envelopes face down grabbed my attention. In a desk where it constantly looked as though a toddler had tossed everything around the order of these envelopes appeared out of place. The fact that they were buried and face down felt ominous and my stomach twisted as I reluctantly reached in to retrieve them. I turned them over in my hands and fingered the address. It was to Robert Warren care of the Georgian State Penitentiary. Most of them were addressed there except the last few. The most haunting one was addressed here, to this address, our street, our apartment. The return address was always the same, no name just 904 Lake Lane in Plenty, Georgia.

My stomach was twisting and my heart was dipping but my brain was trying to calm me. This might be nothing. But then why hadn't he told me about someone in Georgia he had written with, and who was this person? For all I know it could be a priest he met while in jail and continued to confide in. It could be a lot of things because truthfully he rarely talked about the six years he was gone. When he did it always revolved around the photography class and his pictures. I never pushed. I had always assumed he spent his time going through the set regimen, keeping out of trouble, and ticking down the days of his sentence.

Clutching the letters I realized how naive this possibly was. He may have had an entire life down there. I surely did. I finished high school went away to college, partied like all the other students and then was hours away from getting married. What had he done? In the time he had chosen to banish himself what had he been up to? My mind was racing while my fingers opened the envelope and tugged out the first letter. It was crisp and white and well preserved. The words were short and formal. The date lined the top.

December 14, 2001

Dear Robert: Do not write anymore. There is nothing you can do. It is over. Leave this alone. Haven't you hurt us enough?


There was a neatly manicured signature with a large looping S followed by small scribbles that ran together and was impossible to decipher. The following letter gave the same message but with a little more vigor.


February 10, 2002

I implore you to stop writing. We have no desire for your correspondence. We are trying to heal and move on and your insistence on thwarting those attempts are unfair.


The same signature concluded the brief letter. I was reading more but I couldn't figure out what was going on. It all felt so cryptic like *S* had purposely written in a vague manner. The suspense was killing me. I added it to the back of the pile and moved on. This letter looked slightly more worn with the creases broadened and softened from repeated handling.


October 20, 2002

Dear Robert:

The gift is generous. Your adherence to my request of no more letters was appreciated. I am optimistic that time will heal all for her.

My eyes focused on the last word: *her*. It felt as though someone had shoved their hands into my abdomen and were twisting my stomach as though ringing out a sopping wet towel. I could barely swallow. A cry and a scream were hanging on my lips but I was still in the dark and didn't know which one to let escape. Had he been with, liked, or even loved someone in Georgia? Had he smirked at her the way he did me? Teased her and touched her arm? Was *S* this mystery woman? Did he whisper in her ear and tell her intimate things? I felt dirty.

I opened the fourth letter. It almost covered a full page. Surely there would be some answers in here but I was terrified to uncover them.

April 13, 2003

Dear Robert:

I am not sure what all you want to know, what I should tell you, or where I should start. Things have been hard around here. We are trying to move forward and not wallow in the past but it is difficult. Looking at her I can't help but be reminded everyday of the tragedy of it all. It pains me. She has lost so much. There is so much she will never have.

Maybe when she is older I will tell her the whole story but not now. It is impossible. I will not burden her. In the midst of this storm she is the calm center.

Her hair is getting long and it still holds a baby softness and thinness. She is short but her attitude makes up for it. She is the most head strong toddler I have ever met. She runs outside to her cousins each day when they get home from school. She sleeps well, usually straight through the night. Something that took her three older playmates much longer to master. She has a serene nature so maybe it is all related. Her favorite things to do are paint, color, play with stickers, and be read to. She is mastering walking quite well. She is well loved. I am not sure how I feel about writing to you.

The pain that I had felt reading *her* in the previous letter was nothing compared to the deep cut this last letter mangled through my being. My throat was so tight I could barely pass adequate air through the tiny space that remained. My eyes welled with tears as my world, our world, came tumbling and crashing down. Every cell of me was broken and I was left crouching amongst the rubble. Robert and I had twice shared a magnificent life together with the future stretching ahead full of happiness. Both times it was cut short, first by tragedy, and now by betrayal. There was another woman. Another life. A child.

I flashed to hundreds of images of him smiling, laughing, teasing, smirking, tearing, frowning, sleeping, and wondered how could he do those things knowing that it was all a lie. The whole time he was hiding a terrible secret from me. His wife. I had married this man. But I didn't even know him. He was a stranger now. Perhaps he was just a cold hearted man and I had been conned into believing he was a person he merely pretended to be.

I had thought I was so damn lucky to have him. I had thought we loved each other in an exceptional way. It had been like an inside joke between the two of us. Because surely not everyone had been blessed with the intense love we shared. Now I was the joke.

My Robert would never hurt me this way. He was my protector always shielding me. Then I remembered how he lied and let me believe he was dead. How sick and twisted that seemed. How can someone who loves you let you grieve them like I did him? I was in physical pain over his death. I was constantly reminded of his absence. It had been almost impossible getting on with my life after him the first time. I can't do it again. I never got over him. Would it be different this time? Would it be easier knowing he wasn't dead? Or harder? I remembered the pain in my mom's eyes as she watched me waste. How could he do this to me and my family?

Words Troy had said to me when I confessed to him about Robert were trying to break through. I couldn't catch them yet. I thought about Troy and how he had been so patient with me. He had been so persistent about not leaving me alone during my grieving. At first I had been annoyed but then I got used to his company. He didn't make me feel like I needed to go places with him or entertain him. He was content to just keep me company and he let me cry in silence when I needed to. He had been so responsive at reading what I needed. And I had been so quick to leap into Robert's arms when he returned. I turned my back on Troy in a flash and had barely thought about it since. I saw now how horrible that was. I wanted to vomit picturing the last conversation we had had together. The memory overcame me.

After the coffee shop I had driven to our town home. My hands were shaking with nerves as I gripped the steering wheel. I forced myself out of the car and twisted the knob to open the door. Troy was standing in the kitchen fiddling with the coffee pot when I walked in. I could tell he was frustrated and knew that his not knowing where I was for the majority of the day was at least partly to blame. But I had been on the receiving end of that so many times it really shouldn't have bothered me. His worry did bother me though but only because I knew what news was on the horizon for him. We sat across from each other at the dining room table. I was staring at the empty bread basket bracing myself to say the words necessary that would possibly break his heart.

"I don't know how else to say this. Troy, I can't marry you. I am so sorry." I looked up to listen to his response and see his reaction.

He looked utterly confused at first. "What are you talking about? You don't want to marry me?" His voice cracked at the end.

"I am sorry. I just can't. I have been struggling with this for a while"

He cut me off. "For a while? You have been thinking about not marrying me for a while?" He sounded wounded.

"I love you. You have taken wonderful care of me. But I don't love you enough to spend the rest of my life with you." I returned.

"What is going on? What changed?" He was grasping for answers.

"Nothing changed. I just realized that as much as we love each other it's not enough."

"How much *is* enough?" I didn't want to hurt him but I had to tell him the truth, the whole truth.

"I can't love you the way I loved Robert. I don't think I can love anyone that much. I would be lying if I married you because I could never let go of him."

"Sophia, Robert is dead. He is not coming back. You wasted so much time grieving him don't waste the rest of your life now." He tried reasoning with me.

"He isn't dead Troy. He came back…today. He has been in jail this whole time."

"This is ludicrous." He looked at me with disbelief as I knew he would.

I took a few steps backwards and opened the door to let Robert in.

Troy just stared at him.

"It's Robert, Troy. Can you see it's him?" I questioned, surprised he didn't recognize him. My recognition was instantaneous but mom and Troy hadn't seen it. Maybe that was because they hadn't been searching every face on the street for the last six years hoping to find him.

"What?" He relented. Troy's face was full of confusion and anger. He didn't see the connection between Robert's past and our future. I looked at him timidly.

Robert took the reins of the conversation and ran through a simpler version of the well rehearsed story he had told me just hours ago. Was it really only earlier today, I thought unbelievably to myself. Troy seemed to absorb each word at a distance.

"How could you do this? To her? You are so selfish." Troy spit his words in Robert's direction.

"I did what I thought would be best for Sophia at the time. I didn't want her wasting her life waiting for me and I didn't know who I would be after jail. I didn't know if she would want me or if I would be worthy of her." Robert answered.

Troy turned to me completely disregarding Robert. "You don't want to marry me…you don't want this wedding?" He asked me point blank.

"No. I'm sorry. This isn't the right marriage for either of us." I was crying. I could have continued explaining that I had already begun to resent him and that seed would continue to grow over the years making for a melancholy marriage but it was unnecessary to hurt him further. Though I had cried so many times over him I was not vengeful enough to want for him that same sting. I knew that I would quickly forget past pain and I wished for him a similar fate.

"Is he who you want?" He asked disbelieving.

"Yes." I didn't mean for it to come out so devotional but it was unconsciously said in that way.

"I hope that in the future you will see that this was best for Sophia and you." Robert said.

Troy's face reddened and he looked as though his fury was scarcely contained, his fist clenched. "You know you aren't remembering everything about him." He pointed angrily at Robert. "I remember thinking that all those years ago as I rocked, consoled, and held you while you cried over him. You were only remembering the good times. You were quick to forget the bad." He was alluding to something in particular or in general I couldn't tell but it didn't matter. I had expected Troy to be upset and hurt but not to fight for me.

"That is where you are wrong. I do remember." This is one thing I was sure.

He shook his head and looked at me like I was missing something. What did he want from me? To prove my perfect memories? I could tell him how Robert could still revive overwhelming sensations when he touched me, or how I couldn't help beaming like an idiot when our eyes met, or how furious I used to get at him sometimes. The powerful emotions Robert had once and continued to evoke from my being was proof that I remembered and that he was the one without a doubt I was to spend my life with.

There really wasn't much more to say. Troy could shout for

the next couple hours and I could cry but it wasn't going to change what was done. I laid the ring lightly on the table between us and turned to the door.

I came back to the darkness of Robert's office. I managed to pick myself up from the desk chair and crossed the hall. My body was stiff after being in the same position and sore from rocking and tensing as I cried. My fists were clenched tight with my nails digging into the palms and I loosened one hand so I could turn the nozzle for the shower on. I stepped into the water and steam rose off my skin. I hugged my arms to my naked body and let the water run over my head, soak my hair, and pour over my face as I stood unmoving. It rolled down my body and I willed it to wash away the disgusting feeling my skin was giving me as I tried to block out images of all the times Robert had touched me. Eventually exhaustion took over me and I curled into a ball on the shower floor. I was crying again my tears mixing with the water. My defenses were gone. My skin was no longer a barrier. It was scarcely there, merely a translucent layer now. The droplets pelted my skin and I could feel the sting of each one. The water went cold and I reached up and turned it off then lowered myself back into the fetal position on the shower bottom. I was pathetic. I was hiding from the world in my shower. I contemplated nothing for a while. My mind was tired of remembering, imagining, supposing, and when I figured the tank was full of hot water I turned the nozzle on again and let the water assault me once again.

Later I sat at the kitchen table and stared at the glowing red numbers on the stove clock. I am not sure how much I had slept during the night after finding the letters. The hours were blurred by tears. When my body was tired, I would sleep, and then wake and cry some more.

At 9:00 I climbed in to the car and started toward the airport mechanically. My heart for the second time in my life had swelled to capacity with my love for Robert and now it was hemorrhaging with this new pain. I had been so careless to let myself get swept away and now I would pay the price. The tears threatened to spill but I held them back afraid to lose sight of the road. Slowly during the silence in the car my agony became fury. I wanted to scream at the top of my lungs until there was no voice left inside me. I was seething as I stepped out of the car and made my way to the entrance. My hands were balled into fists and pressed firmly into my thighs as I walked in.

I didn't see him until he stepped through security. His eyebrows raised and he smiled but when he took, the most likely hideous picture of me in, his face fell and he headed toward me with concern. Definitely not the reunion he was expecting.

I on the other hand was braced and ready to explode. He had his arms out reaching for me but slightly bent with apprehension. I raised my fists and thrust them at his chest, pounding them into him. I wanted to hurt him physically.

He was stunned and stepped back.

"How could you? You lied to me. Who is she?" I screamed

at him. I didn't care who heard. I was furious. "Who is she? Who is she?" I just kept repeating myself louder and louder.

His hands had fallen to his sides. "Sophia, stop." He took his left hand then slowly with his fingers partially curled in, lifted them toward me. A gesture I knew all too well. He had touched me in this tender way a hundred times.

I yanked my shoulder back harshly knowing he was planning to brush my arm.

"Don't touch me?" I said through clenched teeth with my voice full of hurt and anger.

"What is going on?" He was begging me for information.

"I know about S." I shouted.

"Who?" He seemed so sincere. Damn he was a good actor. If I wasn't 100% sure that he was lying then I would almost believe that he didn't know what I was talking about.

"The mother of your child!" I screamed back.

"What? No, it's not what you think." He looked like an old man all of a sudden. Like he was tired and ready to succumb to death.

"NO?" I reached into my bag pulled the stack of letters out. Before he could react I threw them at the ground. I didn't see them scatter but I heard the smack they made when they hit the ground. My back was already turned and I was darting toward the exit.

He was shouting to me, pleading for me to wait or stop but I refused. Finally he caught up and grasped my shoulder with an iron hold just before I walked through the exit doors.

I reeled around.

He was still fumbling with the letters trying to get them in somewhat of a pile all while looking old and sad. But still not half as bad as I felt. If I didn't hate him so much, I would have laughed at his awkward positioning. Elbows at weird angles, letters jutting out every which way, and a few things held in his teeth. But I did hate him, so it wasn't funny. It fucking sucked. I glared at him with the meanest coldest stare I could muster but it was still nowhere near the fury flaming within me.

"It's not what you think."

"You are a good liar. I guess I shouldn't be surprised though. You have been lying to me since the day you died." That finally crippled him.

His knees bent and the papers fell again.

I turned and walked off without a look back. I realized it was the second time I hadn't looked back when leaving him at the airport.

I drove back to the apartment as though I were on autopilot. When I reached our street, I realized it was the last place I wanted to be and pondered for a second about where to go before I turned in the direction of my parent's house.

No one was home. Thank God. I don't think I could bear telling my mom or dad about all this. I loped up the stairs and walked into my room. It was as though my parents had put caution tape across the entrance the morning I left and hadn't lifted it until some premonition this morning. My room was exactly as it had been in 2001 when I graduated from high school. The chalkboard wall Robert and I had painted was dusty white from all the erasing and rewriting. Robert's handwriting still took up a big section from when he had scribbled one of my favorite quotes from Jane Eyre. It said "Wherever you are is my home-my only home."

Pictures littered the bulletin boards, mirrors, and the back of the door. Jackie and I at a football game, Robert up close, Robert eating ice cream, Robert in front of the igloo we made. He was everywhere. I was having second thoughts about coming home. It was as though he was inescapable. The thought occurred to me; how had Troy been able to stand coming over here when Robert's presence was suffocating the room. He was on every wall. Either he was blissfully naïve or happy to pretend that he and I were happier than we were. I couldn't fault him though because I had done the same thing. I had deluded myself into feigning happiness in my life with Troy. Lying to myself a lot. Telling myself we were in love. How stupid of me then to pretend I could be happy with him and how stupid of me now to let myself believe happiness was mine with Robert this time around. I couldn't think anymore. It felt like my brain would implode and really that would be a gracious end really.

I must have lain on the bed at some point because I woke up later, disoriented to place and time with a fleece blanket covering me. At some point someone had come in and covered me with one of the living room throws. It was dark outside. There was no clock in my room anymore and I had no idea if it was 6 p.m. or 2 a.m.. I rolled over and took stock of myself. My shirt was rumpled and my body was stiff. I crept over to the bathroom and looked in the mirror. I looked bad. Scary bad. My eyes were swollen, my nostrils were an irritated red, and my lips were chapped. Voices carried up the stairs, and I figured that meant it probably wasn't 2 a.m.. I splashed water on my face, but it didn't help me wake up or feel better.

I peered down the stairs like an intruder surveying his surroundings. My mom was hugging my dad from behind while he stood at the stove sautéing what could be ravioli or squash. It was hard to tell from this vantage point. I inhaled, trying to gather courage as I took the last step that was bound to get their attention. It didn't disappoint and they simultaneously turned in my direction.

"What time is it?" I asked groggily.

"It's 6:30, honey. You're going to eat with us, right?" Ugh. I loved her. I gave her such little credit when I was younger, but she was amazing. She didn't ask me why, what, or how. She accepted my presence without inquiry, exactly what I craved. I needed to feel loved, I needed a home cooked meal, and I needed people that would not judge me.

"Yup." I answered simply.

"Daddy is making squash casserole and ham." I hadn't called my dad, Daddy, since I was four but mom had never stopped when she referenced him in my presence. It was as if she had some silent petition going, hoping I would start again. It was annoying sometimes but tonight it was endearing. I was famished and

248

devoured a healthy portion of what was set on the table. Mom and Dad made polite conversation between the two of them so that an awkward silence never set in. I'm really not sure what they discussed. I was still in a daze. I reached for another piece of bread, and my mom instinctively started to pass the butter when I heard a knock on the door. It wasn't loud, but its mere presence was earth shattering. Everyone froze, not sure what to do next. Our perfect dinner charade had been interrupted and we didn't know what part to play next.

"You want me to get it?" my dad asked, ready to be the bouncer for our front door.

Yes, and could you tell him to fuck off please but what came out was "No. I will." I mustered every bit of courage that was scattered in miscellaneous places throughout my body and I opened the door.

Robert was standing there with his body looking limp. I knew it would be him. He was never one to surrender when it came to me. When we were younger I could shout and scream but he would always be there waiting with his arms open to make it all better. I had always loved that about him. It wasn't going to work this time though. A hug or kiss was not going to change the fact that he had been with another woman, touched her, loved her, and had a child with her. A beautiful child with long blonde hair. He looked genuinely surprised that the door had opened. I guess he expected to be rebuffed. He immediately put his hands up, palms out.

"Please, I am begging you give me ten minutes." Tears were

tracing well worn lines down his cheeks. What a pitiful pair we were. And then a sting as I realized that he and I would never be a pair again.

I didn't say anything but took a step back signaling he could come in. He shrugged through the door and glanced at my parents still sitting at the table.

"Well?" I asked curtly. He nodded toward my parents and I stood firm. Whatever he wanted to say to me he would have to say in front of them.

"She is not mine. Kerrin and I were the only survivors of the accident." He paused letting the words click into place in my brain. "S is Sarah, her aunt who took guardianship of her when her sister died in the accident I caused."

I was dumbfounded. I didn't move or speak so he continued.

"I knew I didn't deserve you after the accident when to Kerrin I would always be the monster that took her parents away. I didn't know how to be both people. I pledged myself to making amends for the horror I inflicted and hoped that someday if I succeeded I could come back to you." I pictured him my pillar of strength brought to his knees. "When my photographs started getting popular I knew what to do. I put every cent away for Kerrin and set her up for life. It doesn't take away what I did. I did my best. I did all I could do. Sophia, say something. Please."

My parents had initially tried to eavesdrop nonchalantly but as our conversation deepened, I noticed they were blatantly staring with their mouths practically on the table. They were as blindsided as was I.

"I don't know what to say." I had my arms overlapping across my chest, closing myself off.

"Please tell me it's ok. Tell me that you still love me." He took a small step toward me and I instinctively stepped backwards. Things had changed so fast and so drastically between us.

"I can't right now. I can't." I clumsily shuffled my feet backwards. I didn't want to be here in the middle of the living room with three pairs of eyes staring me down. I climbed the steps two at a time and slammed my door shut behind me, teenager style. I didn't care that I had left my parents down there in the awkward silence with Robert. Maybe they could all just sort it out amongst themselves and tell me how I should feel and what I should do because there wasn't an ounce of strength left inside me to deal with it. I lay there in the silence. It was deafening.

Later, I opened my mind and let all the questions and worry seep into my brain. So he wasn't a father or cheater, ok. He was still a liar. He was doing something good, trying to make amends for the pain he caused, but he had lied to me. Again. Could I trust him after this? Would I always wonder whenever he told me something if it was a partial truth? Could I ever take what he had to say at face value? Could we ever be the same? Did I want to work at it? Should it be this hard? It had seemed so effortless when we were younger, but now I felt worn down and tired. I felt that I was running the last leg of a marathon, everything hurt, and the sidewalk was looking really appealing. I could just stop, sit, and forget all of this. But could I?

I had done it once before after he came back last year. I had been ecstatic to commit myself to him and to us again. We had melded our lives together seamlessly. We had survived and I thought we were stronger than ever because of overcoming the challenge of being torn apart but maybe I was just fooling myself? Perhaps our relationship was built of sand and not stone. I had been able to cup my hands when we were broken the first time and balance the mound alone until he came back a year ago. But now the sand was pouring through my hands. I was letting it stream between my fingers and get blown away by the wind. It seemed easier to just let go.

## Broken

Light was coming in through the blinds, but I didn't have the energy to get out of bed and close them. I just covered my head with the comforter and fell back asleep. I felt sheltered and safe in the artificial darkness. No one could criticize me in here. I was literally hiding from life.

It didn't take me too long to tire of playing the weak, useless, victim. I threw the covers back forcefully and took pleasure in the cool fresh afternoon air that enveloped me. I pulled my legs out from beneath the covers and slammed them down on top. The comforter puffed up in response sending dust particles flying every which way. I didn't have a plan, but I knew I couldn't lie in the fetal position in my circa 2001 room forever so, determined, I stood up and walked into the bathroom. It was a big step, powering through the confusion and pain. I showered, dressed after picking through my mom's closet, and went down for lunch. The house was empty. I was a little surprised, as if I had expected everyone to be frozen in time, with my parents at the table and Robert standing in the foyer with his arms still reaching for me.

I brewed coffee and examined each drop that fell into the pot while I called the school to say I was feeling better and would be back Monday. I called my mom next, knowing she was worried and let her know I was out of bed. She told me my room was always available and I could stay as long as I wanted. She didn't ask me anything or tell me what happened after I abandoned everyone last night and I was glad. I poured the coffee into a travel mug that said "Best Daddy Ever" which meant mom had bought it for dad from me, then grabbed my keys and headed out.

There was a note folded neatly and tucked beneath my wiper blade. It was from Robert.

Sophia: I don't know what to do or say. I don't want to interfere but I want to be there for you. If you will let me. Usually I am not good at giving you space when we are fighting but I understand if that is what you need. I will stay with my parents. I will call you. Call me anytime. I love you.

I threw the car into gear and sped home to the apartment. Even if he wasn't there I still couldn't stay. I tossed armfuls of stuff into my luggage bag and brought piles of clothes to the car still on the hanger. I was determined to get this over with. I didn't want anyone seeing me. I was ready to bawl and/or bite someone's head off. Not a good combination. My vision was tunneled. I was terrified to look at anything besides the carpet and whatever I was grabbing to bring to my parents. Memories threatened me from every angle but I fought them off focusing on the task at hand. It had been twenty minutes of steady work and I was nearly done gathering the essentials so I could move out indefinitely. I was on the last trip, with a mass of clothes still on the hanger piled to my chin. I was trying desperately not to lose anything as I stepped out of the doorway. I couldn't see a foot in front of me because of the towering heap in my arms. I tripped because of course that is what would happen when I was already pissed off.

"What the hell. Goddamn it." Blew out of my mouth before I noticed the small black man sitting in one of the rickety chairs Robert had put on the front porch. We liked to sit there and people watch. Used to, I corrected myself. I was tempted to just bulldoze over him, but Robert's dad looked so innocent, like a small child that needed help finding his dog. His body was conformed into the sagging lawn chair. He had a brown fedora on which added to his harmless appearance. What the hell was he doing here? He had never come to our apartment before.

"Mr. Warren, Robert's not here." I explained.

"I know. I came to talk to you." He sounded composed. Like a preacher prepared to speak a sermon.

I realized then that I had cussed in front of this very church

255

going man. Crap.

"Oh. I'll be right back." I trudged down the steps again and plopped the pile of clothes onto the others, smashing them down so I could close the trunk. My stomach was churning as I ascended the stairs back to where he sat.

"You want to talk to me?" I dragged the other lawn chair out from the side of the house and it screeched along the concrete pad.

"Sophia, I know you thought it was hard when Robert was gone, when you thought he was dead. I would reckon that both of you in your naiveté considered it a great challenge to reconnect when he returned. Yes?"

I nodded in response. Yes, it was a challenge. Was he kidding me? If he was trying to cheer me up, he really sucked at this.

"Truly it wasn't. You had both waited, praying, hoping, begging that you could have one another back again. I assume you did and I know Robert did. He rarely called during those six years, but when he did, he always talked about you. Your reunion was a gift. You were both given what you desperately wanted. Breaking things off with Troy, confiding in friends and family, canceling the wedding that was difficult, but Robert's reemergence in your life was not a problem to deal with. It was a miracle to be thankful for."

"I will not make excuses for him. Sometimes I can't figure him out at all, but this I understand. Robert was ashamed after the accident. Forcing us to pretend he was dead was as much for himself to grieve as us. He truly thought he could never be himself again, that boy was gone. He cut us off too you know. He didn't call us for two years. In reading the letters last night I found it wasn't until after he had given money and Sarah had started to acquiesce that he let us back in. Even then he was very guarded about what he said and our conversations usually revolved around you."

"Trusting him after he kept Kerrin's existence to himself would be a heavy hurdle. I can't imagine the pain you are feeling at being betrayed. I know at this moment you are broken, but it could come to be a legacy of sorts. You have to weather all kinds of conditions in a marriage, but I have faith you two could have an amazing course. Just ask yourself one question, please." He was lifting himself out of the chair, so I stood too. "Is what you had worth fighting for?" A tear came to my eye. He leaned over and embraced me. He had never hugged me before, and it felt good to be accepted by him. His gentle nature had always been evident but I could never really figure him out. His coming here and talking to me spoke volumes. His wife's prejudices were obviously not his own, and I was relieved and grateful.

It was nice to know that I had an ally in their house. I just wasn't sure if it mattered anymore.

"Thank you for coming."

I slumped back into the chair and ran his words through my mind over and over. I could see he was right about Robert coming back. It really hadn't been hard. I had thought before we were warriors that had won a battle and our reward was to keep each other, when really we were more akin to a c      that had gotten lucky by winning the lottery.

Two weeks later I was trying to run. I had been following a trail through the park near my parent's house the last few times because it was shaded and had nice scenery. I liked to hear the twigs crack beneath my feet, and because of all the trees lining the path, I felt alone. I liked to be alone lately. I hadn't had much luck running though. I felt discombobulated. My feet were always a beat off from the arc my arms made in the air. My knees were slightly rubbery, and I couldn't focus on a thought or completely block everything out either. It was frustrating. I just wanted to power through the five-mile course and feel exhausted and simultaneously refreshed. I wanted to see things clearly and know what I should do. I used to do my best thinking when I was running now my thought patterns were all awkward. I was trying to focus on the music pounding in my ears when Robert came to mind as he did a hundred times a day.

He had called that morning. The way he did every morning. He wasn't pushy about me giving him an answer or coming back. He was letting me have space. He just wanted me to know he was there. I looked forward to it more than I liked to admit. He made small talk about what he did the day before, and I listened. I couldn't bring myself to have a conversation, but I liked to hear his voice. He had asked me out on a date for the weekend coming up and I said I would think about it. I thought how we had fallen so far from where we were. Living apart, not seeing each other, having to plan a date. Could we climb out of this hole?

Dinner was probably a good idea. We could feel each other out again. I should say yes. I would tell him tomorrow.

I gave up on the run and started walking the last leg back to the house. His dad's words pierced at my conscious. They had been haunting me lately. "Is what you had worth fighting for?" A simple question with a complicated answer. I had decided there were two answers to that question and was pretty positive that dinner would help me choose one. It was frightening that on one hand the answer was yes and on the other, the answer was no.

If Robert and I could be what we had been, love deeply and recklessly, rely on each other fully, and complete each other. If his presence could still make my heart skip and his smile course warmth through me, than yes, those feelings and desires were worth work, time, and patience to possess again.

But if my vision of him was clouded with bitterness, if our love was forever tainted, if we could never again have the unbounded innocent love we had been so fortunate to enjoy twice in our lives, than no. Living with him, lying beside him, growing old with him would not be worth a mediocre marriage, not when what we had was so amazing. His presence would only serve as a constant reminder of what was lost.

## Dinner

It was Friday night. Date night. It had come up so fast. I was trying to keep my feelings reserved even though I was looking forward to spending a couple hours with Robert. I hadn't seen him in the two weeks since he last came to my parents' house. Our apartment had remained empty during that time. He had been staying at his parents and I at mine. I guess neither of us could bear to be there with our relationship in its current state.

My mom came down the hall as I was laying my keys on the kitchen counter. She and dad had been really great about giving me space to figure things out on my own. Every now and then I would catch them staring at each other trying to communicate solely through their eyes, and I would wonder what they thought of all this. Did they think Robert was a liar? Did they think he had broken the

proverbial last straw?  Did they think I should have married Troy?
And sometimes I wondered briefly if they thought I was being
harsh.  Fortunately they didn't add their opinions to the turmoil that
was already overflowing my brain.  I couldn't handle one more bit
of information to factor into the chaos.  It was like trying to sort
puzzle pieces out so you can assemble the picture but without a
surface to lay them on for organizing.

"A package came for you today.  It's in your room."  She
said indifferently.

I wasn't expecting anything and curiosity forced me to go
straight to my room.

Placed on the center of my bed was a large white box with a
purple bow tied around it.  I was sure immediately it was from
Robert and knew my mom had come to the same conclusion even
though there were no markings on it.  She must have known I would
want to open it in private.

I had no idea what our plans were for the evening just that he
requested I be ready at six.  I had wondered what I should wear but
not knowing what we were doing or where we were going had made
the process doubly challenging.  Of course Robert would have
thought of my quandary and remedied it for me.  I pulled the string
untying the bow and lifted the ribbon off the box.  When I removed
the lid and tissue paper, I saw a beautiful black dress.  It was
sleeveless with a rounded neck, slight empire waist, and tea length.
It was classy.  There were three wide satin ribbons, pink, white, and
red; beneath the dress and a card beside them.

You would look gorgeous in anything but when I saw that this dress offered three different ribbons I knew it was made for you; someone who is both classic and vibrant.

He had always been thoughtful. I had to give him that. Smiling warmly to myself I replaced the card and laid the dress out on my bed. I stood under the warm water for a long while and then took my time doing my hair and makeup. I enjoyed the process of getting ready. My hair was pulled back with some twists and braids into an elegant updo. At quarter to six I slipped the dress over my head and stood in front of the mirror alternating which ribbon I was holding up to it. I was stuck between the soft pink and the red. I chose the red and was trying to tie the bow behind me when the doorbell rang.

*Mom can get it.* I thought to myself. A minute later the doorbell rang again. *What the hell? They must have gone out.* I guess they didn't want to witness what might be a very awkward greeting between their daughter and her husband. If I wasn't so tense, I would laugh at the situation with being picked up at my parents' house and all. It was very reminiscent of our high school dates except we were almost ten years older and married.

I walked down the stairs and opened the door refusing to acknowledge the slight bounce in my step. Robert was beautiful in a black blazer over his white button down and jeans. His cocoa skin smooth and flawless. His head freshly shaved. He smiled wide when he saw I was wearing the dress.

I held up the red ribbon. "I couldn't get it tied by myself."
He took it, and after a couple tries was satisfied it was perfect.

"Thanks." I said simply. It all felt a little surreal. I was so happy he was here. I couldn't deny the butterflies stirring my insides or the smiles we were both trying to subdue. But there was an air of uncertainty that had seeped into our space as well. There had never been something between us like that before and it was sobering.

"Are you hungry?" He asked.

"Famished."

It was natural to let him lead me to the car and close the door for me. I nestled into my side of his car realizing I hadn't sat there in so many weeks. I could tell he had cleaned it for tonight. There were no receipts crammed into the cup holder and the post-its that held ideas, and inspirations, were neatly piled in the middle console.

"Where are we headed?" I asked.

"Dover. Dinner and a show. Sound good?" He questioned.

"Yea. It sounds good. What kind of show?" He was only giving me morsels and I wanted the whole picture. Robert had never taken me to a show before and I was really curious about what he had in mind. Dover was the reluctant capitol of our state. It had the required state buildings but was by no means a center for activity so I was a little worried about what sort of live entertainment he had signed us up for.

"It's a small production of Alice in Wonderland. I don't know. It sounded interesting."

"Yes, interesting is the word I was thinking also." I gave a little humph picturing how a local group would tackle the eccentric tale.

The car fell quiet after that but not an uncomfortable silence. More of a contented silence. We were together, enjoying each other's presence for the first time in a while. I don't think either of us were ready to address the elephant in the room just yet. He tucked his hand beneath my thigh and a tingle rushed through me. I was interested to find that my body still reacted that way to his touch. It made my heart skip and then dip. It would be so easy to be with him but if I *had* to leave I thought about the heart wrenching pain that would fill my future.

He took me to a Thai restaurant that we had talked about going to a few times. After we ordered I needed us to discuss everything. I just didn't know where to begin. If we didn't talk candidly now we would be deliberately ignoring the problem which was something he and I never did. We might shout, scream, and even occasionally talk rationally through arguments but we did not pretend that things were ok between us when they weren't. I was rolling ideas in my mind of how to start while fiddling nervously with my utensils. What did I want to say first? What did I need him to hear? Fortunately he took the first step.

"Sophia, I know I said it before but I am sorry."

I took a deep breath. "But why are you sorry? Are you sorry you got caught?" I pressed.

"I am sorry for everything. For getting in that car when I

shouldn't have been driving, for causing the accident, for having to desert you for so long, for not being completely truthful with you. I had already hurt you so much and when I saw you again that first day in the dress shop. You looked at me like I was a miracle, angel, and hero all wrapped into one. I didn't want to tell you it was a lie. That I was none of those things. You make me wonder if I can be a better person because you see me as someone I am not. But I want to be."

"Robert, you are always trying to protect me. Can't you see now how that has torn us apart time and again. If you had been honest with me about the accident we could have worked it out somehow. If you had told me about Kerrin I would have accepted it. Instead your shielding ends up hurting me. I am not a child, I am your wife." I ended in a stern tone.

"I just want to be what you need. I want to be everything for you." He looked defeated.

"You are. You are everything to me but I have to know I can trust you. That you aren't going to continue keeping things from me in some misguided attempt to protect me. Stop trying to live up to my vision of you. You don't have to. In me you are that person. It's not something you have to work at or become. I see you that way because I love you and you *are* my soul mate. I love that vision because it is you. I don't love you because of that vision. Do you understand?" The words were coming to me quickly. It felt good to tell him these things. He made it easy listening intently and wanting to hear what I was saying.

"I think so. At the same time that you see me different I see you different also. That is why I am always trying to guard you. To me you are innocent and pure and begging to be safeguarded. I want you happy all the time and if I could I would shelter you from anything that might hurt you."

"But you can't. Don't you see that? I need to be your equal. I don't need a guardian. I need a partner. It's like in Jane Eyre when I forget which one says: *You will not exclude me from your confidence, if you admit me to your heart.* You have to be honest with me whether you fear that what you tell me might hurt. You are giving me a false sense of security and now I am paranoid that there are all these secrets you are hiding from me. I have to be able to trust you."

Robert bowed his head as my words hung in the air between us. "I don't want you to worry that I am not being honest. I am telling you now, Sophia, that I vow to be honest with you always. I will not break that promise. Do you believe me?"

"Yes." I did believe him. I knew that he had never meant to hurt me. I knew that the extent he went to protect me was always with the best of intentions. And I knew that he could see now he could not always shelter me. I was sure that our future would not be filled solely by happiness but I knew too that we would share in the pain, fear, and confusion that is inescapable in life.

He leaned over the table awkwardly and touched my face.

I leaned up and we kissed. It was deep and strong with need. Our lips and tongues hadn't touched in this way in far too long and our bodies yearned for their compliment. The kiss could have gone on forever but a ways, in I noted silence surrounded us. Our lips disconnected and we sheepishly noticed other couples with their utensils suspended mid motion.

Robert put his hand up and smiling broke the tension when he said "Excuse us. Sometimes I just can't get enough of my wife."

We laughed a little and so did the other diners.

## Party

The warm breeze was kissing my bare shoulders while I stood elated on our front porch greeting friends and family. I was dressed in a flowing coral sundress with my hair braided down one side. Robert was inside giving Jen and Andy the grand tour. We had worked so hard on crafting the house to our liking and now we were getting to share it with everyone. I had gone crazy in the last week cleaning, decorating, and planning. I wanted it perfect and it was. The floors practically squeaked when guests walked on them. My mom and dad had helped me make all the food. It was picnic favorites. Everything from deviled eggs and potato salad to hamburgers and hot dogs. I had rented a white tent that covered a good portion of the backyard and it was practically ablaze with white Christmas lights. Music was floating up from the patio where a fire was roaring in the pit Robert had built with leftover pavers.

My eyebrows lifted when I saw Jackie's shiny BMW park on the curb. I wasn't expecting her because she hadn't RSVP'd but I hadn't given up hoping she would show. We hadn't spoken since I saw her at the thrift store. I still couldn't understand her distance until I saw the driver climb out of her car. It was Troy. She gave me a guilty shrug when they made it up the walk and I responded with a boisterous hug. How could she think for a second I would be upset over her dating Troy? I would never understand but I planned to berate her for it for years to come. I ushered them inside to poke around and gave them a few directions about the backyard setup.

I saw Robert's parents coming up the walkway next. We all had sincere smiles on our faces and I was glad that his mom, could look at me like that. She and I had bonded some in the last few months and though our relationship wasn't close, we were comfortable around each other and that was plenty. Robert's dad, on the other hand, would always hold a special place in my heart because he had reached out to me and I would be forever grateful for his boldness.

It was hours later, the house tours had been completed and the majority of the food had been consumed. Before cranking the music loud so those brave enough could dance Robert and I called for everyone's attention. I stood holding his arm while he thanked everyone for coming. He explained there was one last addition to the party. We broke from each other and each grabbed one of the oversized iron handles on the barn doors. We walked backwards stretching them wide open and Robert's newest collection of photographs hung from the exposed ceiling beams for everyone to see.

I had been apprehensive at first because they were all of me and mildly sensual but no one could tell. Each was a black and white macro shot and none included my face. My favorite was a close up of my collar bone with one finger delicately smoothing along the shadow on my skin. People started to cross the lawn towards us and I looked over at Robert. He was looking at me and we shared mischievous grins. My throat tightened as emotions overwhelmed me, I was drawn back to one of the early days after he returned to me.


We walked side by side toward the car. We had no destination. I bounced my shoulder onto his and beamed a smile in his direction.

"Did you miss me?" He responded lightly to my tap.

"Just a little." I teased. "So what now?"

"Well, I was thinking happily ever after and all that good stuff." He grinned.

"So, your plan was come back, rid me of my fiancé, sweep me off my feet. Maybe you have served your purpose I could have been using you to get rid of him."

He eyed me incredulously. But I could tell he was thoroughly enjoying the banter.

"Seriously, I just got out of a long term relationship, I don't know if I am ready for more commitment." I harassed.

We chuckled. Robert drove and I didn't ask or care where we were going. It didn't matter. He reached over and put his hand on my thigh. We had gone so long without touching that our bodies automatically reached for the other. It was as though our bodies summoned one another. I had my eyes closed enjoying the warmth and pressure where he touched me and dreamed of all the future days we would have just like today.

**Want more Sophia?  The sequel is set for release SPRING 2016.**

## Email the author for an extra scene

nicolejasonhall@live.com

## You can review this novel at amazon.com

Made in the USA
Middletown, DE
06 July 2015